SpringerBriefs in Political Science

SpringerBriefs present concise summaries of cutting-edge research and practical applications across a wide spectrum of fields. Featuring compact volumes of 50 to 125 pages, the series covers a range of content from professional to academic. Typical topics might include:

- A timely report of state-of-the art analytical techniques
- A bridge between new research results, as published in journal articles, and a contextual literature review
- A snapshot of a hot or emerging topic
- An in-depth case study or clinical example
- A presentation of core concepts that students must understand in order to make independent contributions

SpringerBriefs in Political Science showcase emerging theory, empirical research, and practical application in political science, policy studies, political economy, public administration, political philosophy, international relations, and related fields, from a global author community.

SpringerBriefs are characterized by fast, global electronic dissemination, standard publishing contracts, standardized manuscript preparation and formatting guidelines, and expedited production schedules.

Nina Tynkkynen • Linnéa Henriksson
Björn Egner • Viena Lahtinen
Julia Landrock • Carolina Grönberg

How to Achieve Sustainable Housing?

Insights from Six Cities in Finland
and Germany

Nina Tynkkynen ⓘ
Faculty of Social Sciences
Åbo Akademi University
Turku, Finland

Björn Egner ⓘ
Institut für Politikwissenschaft
Technische Universität Darmstadt
Darmstadt, Germany

Julia Landrock ⓘ
Institut für Politikwissenschaft
Technische Universität Darmstadt
Darmstadt, Germany

Linnéa Henriksson ⓘ
Faculty of Social Sciences
Åbo Akademi University
Turku, Finland

Viena Lahtinen ⓘ
Faculty of Social Sciences
Åbo Akademi University
Turku, Finland

Carolina Grönberg ⓘ
Faculty of Social Sciences
Åbo Akademi University
Turku, Finland

ISSN 2191-5466   ISSN 2191-5474   (electronic)
SpringerBriefs in Political Science
ISBN 978-3-031-86385-1   ISBN 978-3-031-86386-8   (eBook)
https://doi.org/10.1007/978-3-031-86386-8

This work was supported by Technische Universität Darmstadt and Åbo Akademi.

© The Editor(s) (if applicable) and The Author(s) 2025. This book is an open access publication.

Open Access This book is licensed under the terms of the Creative Commons Attribution 4.0 International License (http://creativecommons.org/licenses/by/4.0/), which permits use, sharing, adaptation, distribution and reproduction in any medium or format, as long as you give appropriate credit to the original author(s) and the source, provide a link to the Creative Commons license and indicate if changes were made.
The images or other third party material in this book are included in the book's Creative Commons license, unless indicated otherwise in a credit line to the material. If material is not included in the book's Creative Commons license and your intended use is not permitted by statutory regulation or exceeds the permitted use, you will need to obtain permission directly from the copyright holder.
The use of general descriptive names, registered names, trademarks, service marks, etc. in this publication does not imply, even in the absence of a specific statement, that such names are exempt from the relevant protective laws and regulations and therefore free for general use.
The publisher, the authors and the editors are safe to assume that the advice and information in this book are believed to be true and accurate at the date of publication. Neither the publisher nor the authors or the editors give a warranty, expressed or implied, with respect to the material contained herein or for any errors or omissions that may have been made. The publisher remains neutral with regard to jurisdictional claims in published maps and institutional affiliations.

This Springer imprint is published by the registered company Springer Nature Switzerland AG
The registered company address is: Gewerbestrasse 11, 6330 Cham, Switzerland

If disposing of this product, please recycle the paper.

Acknowledgements

We would like to warmly thank Melina Lehning and Jonas Schauman for their valuable contribution to the *Who Cares About Sustainable Housing?* research (2022–2024).

We are grateful to Turun Kaupunkitutkimusohjelma (The Turku Urban Research Programme) and Länsi-Suomen Yleishyödyllinen Asuntosäätiö (The West Finland Charitable Housing Foundation) for the funding that made our research possible.

We appreciate the interviewees for giving their valuable time to the study and for providing insight into the wicked topic of sustainable housing.

We also want to thank all the reviewers who commented on our work during the research and whose feedback improved our work. We are particularly grateful to Kristine Kern for her comments in the autumn of 2023 and to the anonymous reviewer who provided comments on this manuscript.

Competing Interests The authors have no competing interests to declare that are relevant to the content of this manuscript.

Contents

1 Introduction... 1
2 Housing, Climate, and Their Challenges....................... 9
3 Councillors' Views on Housing and Climate.................... 35
4 Wicked Problems at the Crossroads: Integrating Housing
  and Climate Policy for Sustainable Futures.................... 51
5 Policy Advice... 63

Appendix: City Profiles... 75

Chapter 1
Introduction

1.1 General Introduction

Housing is a key issue when considering sustainability and climate change, forming a so-called wicked problem (Rittel & Webber, 1973) that cannot be addressed without considering the ripple effects across society (Ritchey, 2013). An adequate standard of living is a basic human right (United Nations, 2018), which must therefore be implemented by all levels of the state. Climate change mitigation and adaptation measures are crucial for the future of mankind. Thus, housing and climate policy cannot be considered without each other and have to be solved in an integrated way.

This study focuses on Finland and Germany, where the contributions of housing to the carbon footprint are, respectively, about 25% (Nissinen & Savolainen, 2019) and 13% (UBA, 2023). This creates a critical situation where climate change and its effects on housing must be taken into account. Climate change affects various sectors and should be considered holistically, as it will not only force us to face new risks but also intensifies existing ones (Aleksić et al., 2016, 870). Traditionally, however, the political fields of climate and housing have been quite separate, and their recent intersection has not been very straightforward either (Martín, 2022). This book focuses on the challenge of integrating these two political fields—housing and climate—leaning on the governance of the wicked problems framework (see Sect. 2.1) in the efforts to understand the main challenges of integration.

Sustainable development and climate change have been included in Finnish, German, and overall European politics, especially since the United Nations' 1992 Rio Conference and 1994 Aalborg Charter outlining that municipalities and their citizens have a great responsibility in creating environmental, social, and economically sustainable communities (see European Sustainable Cities, 2024). Different levels of governance increasingly link climate change to housing policy, particularly in how housing policy influences the levels of climate emissions and contributes to climate change adaptation. Through climate emissions and the use of fossil fuels, housing policy can also help to scrutinise the dimensions of social and economic inequality.

Cities play a key role in the green transition as urbanisation is accelerating (United Nations, 2016) and cities are responsible for over 70% of CO2 emissions (IEA, 2021, 97). Municipalities have both an obligation and an opportunity to exert influence on climate change and emission reductions through land use, zoning, or transport planning (Finnish Ministry of the Environment, 2022, 130). As the impacts of climate change are felt mainly at the municipal level and because it is the responsibility of municipalities to respond to them, cities also need to prepare for climate change adaptation. Climate and housing policies do not exist in a vacuum; however, the link between them is not automatic.

One challenge in integrating the two policy sectors is that housing policy traditionally has a national or local policy framework, while climate commitments stemming from the UN conventions and the commitments of the European Union (for example The European Green Deal or Fit for 55) operate within a multi-level governance framework (see Pūķis et al., 2023). Another obstacle is a certain rigidity and slowness of institutions. As such, the role of institutions is to enable and maintain institutional continuity (Matutinovic, 2007). In the case of climate, however, institutions can slow the acute and large-scale changes required by the wicked nature of climate change. Previous research identifies the lack of resources as the biggest obstacle for implementing strategies and making concrete changes in (local) politics (e.g. McLaughlin, 1987). This means especially economic resources, but it is not limited to that: a lack of political resources and knowledge can also be a problem (Martín, 2022, 3). In summary, major institutional, economic, and political changes are needed to achieve the desired action and results in integrating housing and climate policy sectors, which likely requires a broader cultural shift (Jones et al., 2018, 47).

Policies are approved, decisions are made, and their implementation is requested by politicians, making the execution of policies on both housing and climate the result of political priorities. By studying local councillors' views on the topic in three Finnish (Turku, Tampere, and Oulu) and three German cities (Kiel, Mainz, and Wiesbaden), this book provides much-needed insight into local climate policymaking and the integration of housing and climate policies at the local level. The book aims to fill current research gaps by offering new information and policy advice concerning a more cohesive integration of the two fields in the local context of two European countries. At large, the book demonstrates the constitution of a wicked problem from different perspectives of local policymaking and can help in understanding the linkages between various sustainability aspects related to housing and climate. This understanding is crucial for the efforts to integrate complex policy sectors. We approach housing from a broad perspective, linking it not only to the number of dwellings, planning, or construction but also to environments, communities, and transport. Much research has already been executed on the technical aspects of (sustainable) housing (see, e.g., Westerink et al., 2013; Hammad et al., 2019; Solly et al., 2020), so there is a need for a more holistic approach.

Since the study focuses on integrating housing and climate policies at the local level, it seems obvious that we should interview local councillors, ideally from each political party represented in the city councils. For the study, we conducted 30 semi-structured interviews in the Finnish cities of Turku, Tampere, and Oulu and 19 interviews in the German cities of Kiel, Mainz, and Wiesbaden. The interviewees were local councillors with some interest or expertise in housing or urban development. The interview data were accompanied by public policy documents, mostly strategies and programmes, from the city websites. We processed these hundreds of pages of text through qualitative content analysis to provide context for the interview data analysis.

The book is structured as follows: The first chapter offers an outlook on the municipal and political setting of the cities and explains the research methods and materials in more detail. The second chapter examines housing and climate policies as well as their intersection based on the cities' policy documents, whereas chapter three focuses on the councillors' views. The fourth chapter presents analysis within the wicked problem framework, future reflections, and conclusions. The final chapter offers policy advice for a more cohesive integration of housing and climate policies from the perspective of the studied cities. The city profiles in the appendix of the report give an overview of the peculiarities, main housing issues, and main climate issues of each city.

1.2 Municipal and Political Setup

The project studied six cities: Turku, Tampere, and Oulu in Finland and Mainz, Kiel, and Wiesbaden in Germany. In Finland, the capital region was excluded for its exceptional status, which places it in its own category in the Finnish context. The cities chosen in Finland are the three next biggest, and the German cities were chosen to match the properties of the Finnish. For this purpose, three criteria were used, all affecting the housing situation in the city and thus assumably also housing policies in the cities. First, the city sizes were required to be somewhat similar to assure comparability, which translated to approximately 200,000 inhabitants. Second, a similar geographical location was required, in this case their position near the water (sea, river, or other larger bodies of water). Third, the cities were required to have universities and, thus, a large student population. All are growing cities, especially Tampere in Finland and Mainz and Kiel in Germany, which poses major complications for the already challenging housing situation and affordable housing in the future. Each city is introduced separately in the city profiles in the appendix.

The Finnish and German local governments show both similarities and differences. In both countries, the municipalities have a strong self-government (Ladner et al., 2021; Ruge & Ritgen, 2021, 123), guaranteed by the country's constitution. The strong self-government ensures the municipalities room for action in different policy areas. Finnish municipalities have a large number of statutory tasks, which in general is apt to decrease the factual capacity of action, but this does not bother cities of this size.

The city councils exercise the supreme municipal decision-making power, with the number of councillors varying by the number of inhabitants: 67 councillors in Oulu, Tampere, and Turku; 49 in Kiel; 61 in Mainz; and 81 in Wiesbaden. In both Finland and Germany, local councillors are laymen who practice politics alongside their regular work. In general, the council meets once a month. Politicians in executive bodies may feel they are more influential, but this project focuses on councillors because they form the highest political will in the municipality, as well as in policy fields where they are not experts themselves. The municipalities in both countries are free to decide on their political organisation (committees, other bodies) and the municipal administration.

In the context of committees urban planning in Finland is usually organised in committees focusing on urban planning, environment, or construction. The social side of housing was usually considered in committees on social and health care until the reform of the Finnish welfare system, which transferred the responsibility for organising health and social services to a new, regional level from 2023. The municipal responsibility for homelessness and social housing is less clear after the reform; municipalities are supposed to promote facilities but are not responsible for the people affected. The city documents place responsibilities for climate and housing policies to multiple different departments and groups. Tampere, however, is exceptional among the Finnish cities as it has a separate unit for sustainable housing and construction.

In Germany, there are differences with regard to the thematic arrangement and linking of the individual policy areas. The policy areas of housing and climate are not usually organised together in the municipal administration. Housing is often organised in the Department of Social Affairs and/or the Department of Urban Development and Construction, while climate is often part of the Department of Economics or Transport. Wiesbaden can be seen as an example of that by having a Department for "Environment, Economy, Equality, and Organisation", a Department of "Construction and Transport", and a Department of "Social Affairs, Education, Housing, and Integration". Additionally, in the case of Wiesbaden, these departments are headed by different parties due to coalition arrangements.

1.3 Materials and Methods

The first part of the material collection took place in autumn 2022 and involved collecting recent policy documents related to housing and climate policy from city websites. The documents were analysed for content about housing, (sustainable) urban planning and climate policy, as well as intersections of each. The documents were used to create a 41-page comparative table of Finnish and German cities, where different sections of housing and climate policy and intersections of the two were covered.

1.3 Materials and Methods

The second part of the document collection included 49 semi-structured thematic interviews with elected local councillors. The interview structure contained the themes of *housing in your municipality, housing policy, housing policy in your municipality, climate and housing,* and *energy* due to the ongoing energy crisis of 2022 at the time. Questions included but were not limited to:

- *How can the housing situation in your city be characterised? What are the central issues connected with housing in your municipality?*
- *Define housing policy—what is important in (a) housing policy? (A: In general, B: In your municipality, C: For you personally, D: For your party)*
- *To what extent do you combine housing and climate? In policy, in practice? Do you see any results?*

The interviewees were selected based on an interest and expertise in housing or urban development, either in their profession, political career, or both. Potential participants showed a varied level of interest in the study, which posed a challenge for achieving a balanced mix of interviewees from different political parties, age groups, and genders. The interviewees were informed about the purpose of the study, their rights before, during and after the interview, and the processing, anonymisation and storing of the data.

In Finland, 30 interviews with local councillors were arranged between January and March 2023; 10 interviewees were recruited in each city, including 18 men and 12 women. The representation of parties varied slightly based on the party map of the cities; for example, in Oulu, more councillors from the Centre Party were interviewed than in other cities. The interviews were between 31 and 63 min; five interviews were conducted via Zoom and the rest face-to-face.

A total of 19 interviews were conducted in Germany between January and May 2023. In general, there was some trouble recruiting interviewees. It was not possible to find a representative from each party in every city, so two representatives were interviewed from the same party in three instances (Mainz: Green Party and Christian Democrats; Kiel: Social Democrats). Some parties refused to participate or never responded to the interview requests.

German interviews were held primarily with councillors who were active within the political field of housing (and not in the field of climate policy), for example by being a member of the housing committee of the city. In the end, six interviews were conducted in Kiel, eight in Mainz and five in Wiesbaden. Of the 19 interviewees, 13 were men and 6 were women. All interviews were conducted via video calls, and they were 45 min long on average.

In total, eight German and seven Finnish parties were included in the study (see Table 1.1). All interviews were recorded, transcribed, and anonymised. The interviews offered a valuable opportunity to see how councillors' views are related to strategies and political documents they have been part of shaping.

Qualitative content analysis was used to find themes, similarities, and differences in relation to (sustainable) housing, climate policy, and the integration of the two. The raw data of the interviews were divided into themes which constitute a basis for the third chapter.

Table 1.1 Party distribution of the interviewees

Finland		Germany	
National Coalition Party	6	Social Democrats	4
The Green League	6	Green Party	4
Social Democratic Party	5	Free Democrats	3
Left Alliance	4	Christian Democrats	3
Finns Party	4	Volt Party	2
Centre Party	4	The Left Party	1
Swedish People's Party	1	Kiel Local Party	1
		Ecological Democratic Party	1
Total	30		19

References

Aleksić, J., Kosanović, S., Tomanović, D., Grbić, M., & Murgul, V. (2016). Housing and climate change-related disasters: A study on architectural typology and practice. *Procedia Engineering, 165*, 869–875. https://doi.org/10.1016/j.proeng.2016.11.786

European Sustainable Cities. (2024). *Aalborg 1994*. Sustainable Cities Platform. Retrieved October 11, 2024, from https://sustainablecities.eu/conferences/aalborg/

Finnish Ministry of the Environment. (2022). *Keskipitkän aikavälin ilmastopolitiikan suunnitelma – Kohti hiilineutraalia yhteiskuntaa 2035 [Medium length climate policy plan – Towards a carbon neutral society 2035]*. Ympäristöministeriön julkaisuja 2022:12. Finnish Ministry of the Environment. Retrieved December 8, 2023, from https://julkaisut.valtioneuvosto.fi/bitstream/handle/10024/164186/YM_2022_12.pdf?sequence=4

Hammad, A., Akbarnezhad, A., Haddad, A., & Vazquez, E. (2019). Sustainable zoning, land-use allocation and facility location optimisation in smart cities. *Energies (Basel), 12*(7), 1318. https://doi.org/10.3390/en12071318

IEA – International Energy Agent. (2021). *World energy outlook 2021*. Retrieved December 9, 2024, from https://iea.blob.core.windows.net/assets/4ed140c1-c3f3-4fd9-acae-789a4e14a23c/WorldEnergyOutlook2021.pdf

Jones, C. M., Wheeler, S. M., & Kammen, D. M. (2018). Carbon footprint planning: Quantifying local and state mitigation opportunities for 700 California cities. *Urban Planning, 3*(2), 35–51. https://doi.org/10.17645/up.v3i2.1218

Ladner, A., Keuffer, N., & Bastianen, A. (2021). *Local Autonomy Index in the EU, Council of Europe and OECD countries (1990-2020)*. European Commission. Retrieved December 8, 2024, from https://ec.europa.eu/regional_policy/sources/policy/analysis/KN-07-22-144-EN-N.pdf

Martín, C. (2022). Exploring climate change in US housing policy. *Housing Policy Debate, 32*(1), 1–13. https://doi.org/10.1080/10511482.2022.2012030

Matutinovic, I. (2007). An institutional approach to sustainability: Historical interplay of worldviews, institutions and technology. *Journal of Economic Issues, 41*(4), 1109–1137. https://doi.org/10.1080/00213624.2007.11507089

McLaughlin, M. W. (1987). Learning from experience: Lessons from policy implementation. *Educational Evaluation and Policy Analysis, 9*(2), 171–178. https://doi.org/10.2307/1163728

Nissinen, A., & Savolainen, H. (2019). *Julkisten hankintojen ja kotitalouksien kulutuksen hiilijalanjälki ja luonnonvarojen käyttö-ENVIMAT-mallinnuksen tuloksia [The carbon footprint and use of natural resources of public purchases and domestic consumption - Results of ENVIMAT-model]*. Suomen ympäristökeskuksen raportteja 15/2019. Suomen ympäristökeskus

References

SYKE. Retrieved December 12, 2024, from https://helda.helsinki.fi/server/api/core/bitstreams/2a58d55b-0006-4413-b2c7-22310fc4c575/content

Pūķis, M., Bičevskis, J., Gendelis, S., Karnītis, E., Karnītis, Ģ., Eihmanis, A., & Sarma, U. (2023). Role of local governments in Green Deal multilevel governance: The energy context. *Energies (Basel), 16*(12), 4759. https://doi.org/10.3390/en16124759

Ritchey, T. (2013). Wicked problems. *Acta Morphologica Generalis, 2*(1).

Rittel, H. W., & Webber, M. M. (1973). Dilemmas in a general theory of planning. *Policy Sciences, 4*(2), 155–169.

Ruge, K., & Ritgen, K. (2021). Local self-government and administration. In S. Kuhlmann, I. Proeller, D. Schimanke, & J. Ziekow (Eds.), *Public administration in Germany* (pp. 123–141). Springer Nature. https://doi.org/10.1007/978-3-030-53697-8

Solly, A., Berisha, E., Cotella, G., & Rivolin, U. J. (2020). How sustainable are land use tools? A Europe-wide typological investigation. *Sustainability (Basel, Switzerland), 12*(3), 1257. https://doi.org/10.3390/su12031257

UBA – Umweltbundesamt. [Federal Environment Agency]. (2023). *Energiebedingte Emissionen von Klimagasen und Luftschadstoffen.* [*Energy-related emissions of greenhouse gases and air pollutants*]. Retrieved December 14, 2023, from https://www.umweltbundesamt.de/daten/energie/energiebedingte-emissionen#entwicklung-der-energiebedingten-treibhausgas-emissionen

United Nations. (2016). *The world's cities in 2016.* Data booklet. Retrieved December 12, 2024, from http://www.un.org/en/development/desa/population/publications/pdf/urbanization/the_worlds_cities_in_2016_data_booklet.pdf

United Nations. (2018). *Universal Declaration of Human Rights at 70: 30 articles on 30 articles – Article 25.* Retrieved December 12, 2023, from https://www.ohchr.org/en/press-releases/2018/12/universal-declaration-human-rights-70-30-articles-30-articles-article-25

Westerink, J., Haase, D., Bauer, A., Ravetz, J., Jarrige, F., & Aalbers, C. B. E. M. (2013). Dealing with sustainability trade-offs of the compact city in peri-urban planning across European city regions. *European Planning Studies, 21*(4), 473–497. https://doi.org/10.1080/09654313.2012.722927

Open Access This chapter is licensed under the terms of the Creative Commons Attribution 4.0 International License (http://creativecommons.org/licenses/by/4.0/), which permits use, sharing, adaptation, distribution and reproduction in any medium or format, as long as you give appropriate credit to the original author(s) and the source, provide a link to the Creative Commons license and indicate if changes were made.

The images or other third party material in this chapter are included in the chapter's Creative Commons license, unless indicated otherwise in a credit line to the material. If material is not included in the chapter's Creative Commons license and your intended use is not permitted by statutory regulation or exceeds the permitted use, you will need to obtain permission directly from the copyright holder.

Chapter 2
Housing, Climate, and Their Challenges

2.1 Housing as a Wicked Problem

Housing, as many other societal policy problems and challenges faced today, is characterised by complex relationships and factors that directly or indirectly affect each other (e.g. Lawrence, 2017). Analysing and understanding such problems requires a holistic and systemic approach and an innovative framework that accounts for not only social or ecological aspects but also economic and cultural aspects of housing (e.g. Smets & van Lindert, 2016; Adabre et al., 2022). One holistic framework is provided by literature focusing on the governance of wicked problems. Rittel and Webber (1973) suggested the concept of wicked problems to refer to issues, including public policies for housing, that require analysis based on multiple angles and values linked to a variety of actors in contrast to "tame natural science problems" that can be solved within the existing modes of knowledge and decision-making. Wicked social science problems have been described in terms of the following ten characteristics (see also, e.g., Head, 2019; Lönngren & Van Poeck, 2021):

1. *There is no definitive formulation of a wicked problem.*
2. *Wicked problems have no stopping rule, i.e. there is no point in time at which the process of addressing a problem is completed.*
3. *Solutions to wicked problems are not true-or-false, but good-or-bad.*
4. *There is no immediate and no ultimate test of a solution to a wicked problem.*
5. *Every solution to a wicked problem is a "one-shot" operation.*
6. *Wicked problems do not have an enumerable (or exhaustively describable) set of potential solutions, nor is there a well-described set of permissible operations for addressing wicked problems.*
7. *Every wicked problem is essentially unique.*
8. *Every wicked problem can be considered to be a symptom of another problem.*
9. *The existence of a discrepancy representing a wicked problem can be explained in numerous ways. The choice of explanation determines the nature of the problem's resolution.*

10. *The planner has no right to be wrong.* (Rittel & Webber, 1973, 161–166)

Research outlines that addressing wicked problems requires collaborative, adaptive governance arrangements that acknowledge the complexity of the issues (see Head & Alford, 2015). This type of governance involves experimenting with policies, learning from outcomes, and engaging diverse stakeholders in dialogue and problem-solving on a continuous basis (e.g. Kettl, 2009; Termeer et al., 2015). Importantly, any intervention must balance short-term needs with long-term sustainability, equity, and resilience.

The concept of wicked problems has been criticised for different reasons, including the assumption that wicked and tame problems would fundamentally differ from each other (e.g. Turnbull & Hoppe, 2019; Alford & Head, 2017) and for the imprecise analytical character that has resulted in "conceptual stretching" of the theory (e.g. Peters & Tarpey, 2019). It has also been argued that the idea is often used as a rhetorical tool to pursue certain political agendas and draw attention and resources to a specific problem (e.g. Peters, 2017), or even to paralyse and exclude stakeholders from addressing these problems (e.g. Noordegraaf et al., 2019). A recent review of the wicked problems literature found that even if the literature is highly dispersed across disciplines and institutions, the term lacks conceptual clarity and cohesion; thus, researchers have difficulties in clearly positioning their work in relation to the broader body of research on wicked problems (see Lönngren & Van Poeck, 2021).

Despite the criticism, we lean on the wicked problems framework here as it promotes a shift from siloed approaches to more systemic thinking, acknowledging the interconnectedness of housing markets, environmental sustainability, social equity, and climate resilience. In brief, housing can be described as a wicked problem due to its complexity, interconnectedness with other societal challenges, and the lack of a clear or singular solution. The housing market and related policies are affected by rapidly changing economic conditions, demographic shifts, migration patterns, technological advances, and changes not only in adjacent policy areas (e.g. regulation of construction) but also in more distant realms (e.g. changes in investment strategies, availability of construction resources and human workforce, etc.). This hampers efforts to predict outcomes or create stable long-term strategies, as interventions must often be reassessed and adapted (cf. Termeer et al., 2015). Furthermore, housing problems are intertwined with issues like economic inequality and social justice, land use and environmental concerns, and challenges related to infrastructure (e.g. Martinez, 2020; Tayefi Nasrabadi et al., 2024). Addressing one aspect, for example increasing housing supply, can affect other aspects, such as affordability or environmental sustainability (e.g. Adamkiewicz et al., 2011; Martinez, 2020; Lima, 2021). Balancing the need for development with protection for vulnerable communities is a persistent dilemma. Therefore, solutions to housing problems cannot be implemented without considering their effects across society (e.g. Ritchey, 2013).

Moreover, housing is not only a technical or economic issue but also a deeply value-laden and politically charged topic. Different actors—homeowners, renters, developers, policymakers, community activists, and environmental advocates—have diverging views, and often conflicting interests, on the subject matter (e.g.

Crabtree & Hes, 2009; Berardi, 2013; Andelin et al., 2015; Herazo & Lizarralde, 2016; Storbjörk et al., 2019. For example, developers might prioritise profitability, while residents seek affordability and stability, which makes it difficult to find solutions that satisfy all parties. Perspectives on what is considered "adequate" or "fair" housing are influenced by cultural and ideological beliefs, making it hard to reach consensus (see Chiu, 2004). Further, housing policies are shaped by historical decisions that can constrain current and future choices. Thus, historical injustices must be considered in contemporary solutions (Callewaert, 2002). Housing policymaking can thus easily become a battleground for broader debates on urban planning, economic development, and social justice, for example.

One of the main characteristics of wicked problems is that they lack definitive or absolute solutions. Housing policies often result in compromises that may solve some issues while exacerbating others; for example, building more social housing in one place risks lower attractiveness for investments in the area and prevents the much-needed mix of social groups in the neighbourhood. Additionally, solutions may vary greatly depending on local contexts and can require continuous adjustments over time. What may be a suitable solution in one context, e.g. in one city, may not work in another city due to variation in context or historical development.

Consequently, the wicked problems framework highlights the inherent complexity of housing, involving various stakeholders, conflicting priorities, and interactions across different sectors and scales. It pinpoints that these challenges cannot be solved with straightforward, one-size-fits-all solutions but that they require trade-offs; well-meaning policies can also have unintended consequences. Acknowledging the wickedness may help policymakers and planners recognise the importance of integrating multiple perspectives and disciplines, promoting more comprehensive and cautious policy development.

In this book, we scrutinise the challenge of integrating housing and climate policies at the local level. Climate change can be considered even a super wicked problem (see Levin et al., 2012), which adds layers of complexity, risk, cost, technology, and social impacts to the wicked problem of housing. Climate change amplifies existing challenges, for example by increasing the vulnerability of housing infrastructure particularly in areas already prone to risks such as flooding or heat waves. Financial pressures related to climate measures often translate into higher housing costs, further exacerbating the affordable housing crisis. Solving one problem (e.g. reducing carbon emissions) may exacerbate another (e.g. increasing housing costs) (e.g. Sovacool et al., 2019; Sharifi, 2020), and solutions cross different sectors involving a mix of environmental, economic, and social dimensions (e.g. Mulliner et al., 2013; Bibri & Krogstie, 2020; Syed Jamaludin et al., 2020; Winston, 2022; Adabre et al., 2022). Together with the evolving nature of climate impacts, this means that housing solutions must account for more than just shelter; they must mitigate risks and build resilience while simultaneously supporting social cohesion (e.g. Hayles & Dean, 2015). Decisions involve long-term planning, but their impact may not be fully understood for decades. Predictions about future resource availability, technology, and climate are inherently uncertain, making it difficult to design robust solutions today (Dobes, 2008; de Wilde et al., 2008). The wicked problems framework enables treating complex and interdependent challenges of housing and climate in an interconnected manner.

2.2 On Sustainable Housing

With the Brundtland Commission's report *Our Common Future*, sustainable development became more widely discussed and defined. It can be understood as seeking to meet the needs of present generations without sabotaging the needs of future ones (WCED, 1987). Sustainability itself is often divided into different dimensions (or "pillars"), the demands of which must be addressed to reach holistic sustainability (Egner, 2023, 16). A distinction is made between the ecological, economic, and social dimensions, with cultural, institutional, and (material-)technological dimensions increasingly appearing alongside them.

Despite the many alternatives, there is no single, agreed-upon definition of sustainable housing (Lovell, 2004, 36). The concept and content of sustainability has proved to be a source of conflict among the various actors in urban development (Hagbert & Femenías, 2016, 2). Given the burden construction and housing place on ecological sustainability, sustainable housing and its pursuit should be further explored.

Seyfang (2010, 7626) has depicted how the rise of the environmental movement in the 1970s increased interest in sustainable housing, which was further affected by the oil crisis (see, e.g., Schramm, 2024) and, consequently, the pursuit of energy efficiency. Sustainability was particularly linked to the waste of materials and energy in the construction methods and technologies of the time. With the passing of the 1970s oil crisis, governments and mainstream developers no longer saw sustainable housing as a motivating factor.

The construction and housing sectors are being driven towards a more sustainable future through incentives, regulation, and innovation (Hagbert & Femenías, 2016, 2). The construction industry is increasingly integrating environmental considerations into its strategies and working practices (e.g. Gluch et al., 2014; Sev, 2009). This is also encouraged by the European Union's collective climate targets. Despite these measures, the urgency of making more climate-resilient housing is clear (Seyfang, 2010, 7624).

Housing is undeniably linked to each dimension of sustainability. The construction process with materials and techniques, the location of construction with transport solutions, or housing itself with energy and water consumption all place a significant burden on the *environment* (Winston & Eastaway, 2008, 213–214; Egner, 2023, 16–17). The *social* dimension can be linked to housing affordability (e.g. Granath Hansson, 2020), accessibility (e.g. Jonsson et al., 2021), or diversity in terms of housing and ownership types (Bramley & Power, 2009). Housing should also be managed in a way that does not abandon *economic* wellbeing, yet does not negatively impact other dimensions of sustainability. Investors, governments, and

2.2 On Sustainable Housing

cities also connect housing to economic sustainability; the sector is vulnerable to various crises and external factors, such as changes in labour markets or accelerating urbanisation (Egner, 2023, 17).

According to Moser (2010), climate change has been a matter of public concern particularly since the 1980s. Despite the continuing acceleration, political action is still insufficient to meet the urgency of climate change. The reasons for this delay include the uncertainty and complexity of the situation, intersecting interests, and insufficient signals of the needed change. Climate change is also inextricably connected with housing, as demonstrated by the close link between housing and ecological sustainability. Constructing a single and precise definition of climate-proof housing faces the same challenges as defining sustainable housing. It can be considered to include smart homes that optimise energy use (e.g. Maalsen, 2020), low- or zero-carbon homes (e.g. Martiskainen & Kivimaa, 2018), housing solutions built from recycled building materials (see *circular economy*, e.g. Marchesi et al., 2020) or housing and neighbourhood solutions that involve car sharing or other common-use arrangements (e.g. Wang et al., 2021). It is not just the dwelling itself that weighs on emissions or climate resiliency, but also its location, the community and infrastructure around it, the distances and how they are covered, and the quality of construction (Winston, 2014, 1386).

We focus on the ecological and, above all, the climate-proof aspect of housing in this book, without neglecting its connections with the other dimensions of sustainability. However, sustainable housing should not be limited only to environmental aspects. We therefore aim to have a more holistic view of housing, including the environment, communities, and transport—but also its sustainability—without sacrificing other aspects for the sake of our climate perspective. As Moore and Doyon (2023, 2) argue, in addition to technical and climate change mitigation benefits, ecologically sustainable housing can also impact other sustainability dimensions in the form of reducing the cost of living and improving health and wellbeing. Sustainable housing is linked to other sectors and innovations to build the most functional and climate-resilient housing possible.

It is clear that sustainable housing, which pursues climate mitigation and adaptation, faces a number of challenges. A major challenge is energy, not only in terms of achieving energy efficiency in the construction and housing phases but also in relation to issues such as the level of consumption (Hagbert & Femenías, 2016). In addition to energy efficiency in construction and housing, *how* energy is brought into homes is not irrelevant; renewable solutions such as solar and wind power are on the rise (EEA, 2024). Fossil fuels are not a sustainable way of producing heat and energy, and solar photovoltaic systems, for example, are growing rapidly in Germany, Spain, and Australia (Moore & Doyon, 2023, 72), indicating an interest in building a future based on sustainable energy. As well as being an embodiment of ecological sustainability, energy is also linked to social wellbeing through energy poverty (e.g. Willand & Horne, 2018).

An increasing number of extreme weather events and other changes require adaptation, making climate change a major theme in sustainable housing. The effects and changes will vary locally, but some notable risks to housing and construction in Europe include hotter summers and the urban heat island effect (e.g. Rubaszek et al., 2021; Herath et al., 2024), milder winters and increased rainfall (e.g. Hayles et al., 2022), or flood risks (e.g. Storbjörk & Hjerpe, 2022; Mariano & Marino, 2023). This can mean, for example, reconsidering the relationship between cooling and heating (see Lahdensivu et al., 2023).

Sustainable housing is also linked to other urban development, infrastructure, compact urban structure, and transport. Erecting housing near public transport and services (Winston, 2014, 1386) or the possibilities of redensification are emerging as important instruments. Redensification, however, also raises concerns among researchers; while it improves access to services, it can affect neighbourhood wellbeing (e.g. Bramley & Power, 2009), and while it is more ecologically sustainable by reducing distances and building in an already "touched" environment, its challenges and trade-offs need to be faced (e.g. Artmann et al., 2019).

In addition to the location and energy efficiency of housing, there are several sustainability issues related to the construction and planning phases. These include but are not limited to the size of dwellings (e.g. McKinlay et al., 2019), preparation of the soil (e.g. Minixhofer et al., 2022), and the use of most sustainable materials and their recycling (e.g. Takano et al., 2014; Taylor et al., 2023). Housing should be designed to be long-lasting and sustainable throughout its life cycle, which requires high standards of design and quality (Moore & Doyon, 2023, 64). However, at some point, many buildings must face the demolition/refurbishment dilemma, in which case the sustainability of the choice at hand must be realistically measured (e.g. Power, 2010).

As this chapter illustrates, holistically sustainable and climate-proof housing is under pressure from a variety of factors. The stakeholders' conflicting values and priorities challenge achieving holistically sustainable housing; reconciling these needs inevitably leads to complications and trade-offs, and improvements in minimum performance requirements or low-carbon targets for sustainable housing are often resisted by key stakeholders (Moore & Doyon, 2023, 101). Sustainable housing involves a wide range of actors, including local and national policymakers, developers, researchers, communities, and residents themselves. It is essential to find a balance between informed decision-making, the right amount of political guidance for construction, the markets, and the responsibility of homeowners. One of the complexities of organising sustainable housing is not only balancing the different interests and needs of the stakeholders but also navigating the interconnectedness of different sectors.

Sustainable housing as a whole can be seen as a wicked problem, with its smaller inner wicked issues, such as homelessness, accessibility, affordability, or environmental sustainability. Efforts to address today's issues, which are tied to our holistically sustainable future, are all the more necessary—not least because we are facing a very time-sensitive climate crisis.

2.3 Description of Policy Systems

2.3.1 Housing Policy

In Finland, municipalities are legally obliged to "improve housing conditions to ensure that everyone has access to decent housing" (Act on Developing Housing Conditions, 1985/919). Nationally, housing is governed by a housing policy development programme. The housing policy targets for 2021–2028 focus particularly on affordable housing and developments on stable prices, adequate housing for groups with special needs, the vitality of areas, and socially sustainable and inclusive neighbourhoods. The targets also mention that construction and housing should be sustainable, considering the emissions (Government of Finland, 2021).

Housing policy in Finland is, inter alia, implemented through cooperation between the state and the municipalities. The state, large cities and the state-subsidised building stock of the Housing Finance and Development Centre of Finland (ARA) cooperate through Agreements of Land Use, Housing, and Transport (so-called MAL agreements). The state also collaborates with municipalities on homelessness, housing for the elderly and the suburban development programme, which aims to make neighbourhoods less segregated. Each Finnish city in the study also participated in the Sustainable City programme (2019–2023), which aimed to spread good sustainability practices through cooperation between municipalities, ministries, and other organisations.

Municipalities are responsible for zoning and land planning, which should aim to prevent segregation. Municipalities also recognise the intersection of social and housing policy, including meeting the housing needs of special groups (Kuntaliitto, 2015). Through the close links between municipal housing and land policies, transport planning and services, these instruments can prevent housing-related challenges such as homelessness or segregation (Antikainen et al., 2020, 5). The three main instruments used by municipalities to control the type and location of construction are zoning, land transfer agreements, and land use agreements. Through zoning and land transfer agreements, municipalities can influence, for example, the size of apartments or what is built on the municipalities' land (Karikallio et al., 2019, 22). Most municipal housing associations in Finland are municipally owned companies; they consider the social and affordable side of housing, and their tasks lie in the construction, management, administration, and marketing of their residential properties.

The current Finnish government (2023–) wants to form a bigger picture of housing, land use, construction, and transport that promote sustainable development. The government programme emphasises that competitiveness and vitality require a functioning housing market and that sustainable development should be pursued through housing as well (Government of Finland, 2023a, 115). The programme calls for sufficient, diverse, and affordable housing but places more reliance on free market construction, as the ARA construction is to be moderately reduced. Like the previous government, the current one also aims to eliminate long-term homelessness by 2027 (ibid., 121–122). A new Building Act entering into force in 2025 will strive to comprehensively consider climate change and the circular economy in relation to construction and land use (Finnish Ministry of the Environment, 2023a).

In Germany, the municipalities also play an important role within the policy field of housing, similar to Finland with regard to the provision of housing for low-income people and the creation of new housing in general. In addition to the municipalities, however, the national level is also involved in housing policy and formulates major targets. Housing policy issues are divided between the national level, the level of the federal states (German *Länder*), and the level of the municipalities. While the national level focuses on the superior housing policy targets, the 16 Länder are generally entrusted with implementing and executing federal laws. The states are also responsible for organising social housing and applying the regulation of construction as well as the regional planning and social housing. Municipalities and counties at the local level are responsible for the administration of building land development and construction rights (Egner et al., 2018, 8; Krapp et al., 2021, 92).

Local authorities in Germany are, as in Finland, free to decide how they organise themselves regarding the local municipal administration (Rink & Egner, 2020, 28), yet there are several differences regarding the location of housing policy issues within the local administration. Mostly, they have a housing department (Wohnungsamt), or housing issues are shared between different parts of the administration (Krapp et al., 2021, 92).

Municipal housing associations (companies)—like in Finland—play an important role within the German local housing policy, particularly in creating affordable housing. These municipal housing associations can be involved in the construction of apartments financed by social housing subsidies. If this is the case, the apartments are tied to certain rental prices and occupancy rates. In addition to municipal housing associations, there are a large number of other housing policy stakeholders at the local level, and these have been described as a "field of tension between different interests" (Krummacher, 2011, 204). Since selling a huge part of the non-profit public housing sector in the 1980s, when the need for affordable housing "was temporarily perceived as less urgent" (Richter, 2023, 80), local authorities are limited in their ability to control local housing policy. This poses challenges for municipalities, particularly in providing affordable housing for economically disadvantaged people. Now, the allocation of new subsidised housing, which is built as part of social housing, is one of the main powers of the municipalities to influence local housing policy.

Further, the local level focuses on the administration of construction rights and building land development. Municipalities are also in charge of the administration and payment of housing allowances/benefits to financially disadvantaged people (paid for by the federal and the federal state level). Local authorities can voluntarily take over the calculation of the local rent index. Their responsibility also includes accommodating for refugees, which has been a major challenge for local authorities since 2015.

2.3 Description of Policy Systems   17

According to the coalition agreement of the German federal government taking office in 2021, future housing and construction should be affordable, climate neutral, sustainable, barrier free, and innovative (Bundesregierung, 2021, 88). This should be achieved under the consideration of the diverse contributing factors, ways of living, and individual needs of the inhabitants. The German government aims to address urban as well as rural communities. The coalition agreement envisions a fundamental shift in Housing, Construction, and Urban Development Policy. One of the main targets is the construction of 400,000 new apartments per year (ibid., 88), with a quarter being subsidised by governments. Regarding the social aspects of housing policy, an "Affordable Housing Alliance" should also be established with all relevant stakeholders. A building, housing, and climate check is also to be introduced. In addition, local authorities are to be supported in the introduction of a new register, which should list the potential of available building grounds in the urban area (ibid., 89). But housing is not only considered an important topic for national politics. In a recent survey among German mayors, housing was mentioned as the no. 3 priority (Difu, 2022).

2.3.2 Climate Policy

Finland aims to be carbon neutral by 2035 and has set several emission reduction targets to be achieved between 2030 and 2050. By 2050, Finland aims to reduce emissions by 95% compared to the levels of 1990 (Finnish Ministry of the Environment, 2023b). The Finnish Climate Act includes a long-term climate plan, an adaptation plan, a medium-term climate plan, and land use sector climate plan. To enable a just transition, Finland has adopted concrete measures such as subsidies for switching to a more ecological form of heating and support for the construction of charging points for electric cars (Finnish Ministry of the Environment, 2022a). Much of Finland's climate policy is influenced by climate and energy obligations, policy decisions and legislation of the European Union. The state also offers resources for tackling climate change, for example in the form of economic resources for renewable/sustainable energy solutions or sustainable transport projects (Finnish Ministry of the Environment, 2022b, 3).

The state and municipalities cooperate in climate policy via funding, various projects, and agreements that create and maintain sustainability in municipalities. Practicing climate change adaptation side by side with mitigation at national, regional, and local levels has been increasingly highlighted (Hildén et al., 2022). According to the 2021 survey by the Association of Finnish Municipalities, a large proportion of the surveyed municipalities also cooperate to achieve climate targets, but some difficulties were reported between municipal and regional cooperation (Puurula et al., 2022, 21).

In general, Finland has a strong self-government, and municipalities are responsible for their own climate policies on areas such as zoning, land use, traffic planning, ownership of energy companies, et cetera (Finnish Ministry of the Environment,

2022c, 137). Thus, municipalities hold both an opportunity and an obligation to contribute to climate change mitigation and adaptation through the emissions of the municipal organisation, as well as its citizens and businesses. In larger cities, climate and environmental issues are often briefly mentioned in other policy documents, such as city strategies, in an attempt to include a climate perspective across the political spectrum. Finnish municipalities generally have their own separate strategies for climate change and environment. Among the municipalities, 138 have their own carbon neutrality goal, with larger municipalities naturally more likely to have one. Municipalities mostly focus on mitigation rather than adaptation in their climate policy. The possible lack of a strict climate policy in municipalities is usually connected to the lack of resources or politicians' interest and the polarised nature of the climate debate (Puurula et al., 2022).

Finnish municipalities have been proactive in pursuing carbon neutrality, even by international standards (Seppälä et al., 2019, 28–29). In the 2000s, Finland saw the growth of several national climate networks, such as HINKU (Towards Carbon Neutral Municipalities) and FISU (Finnish Sustainable Communities), which have led municipalities towards carbon neutrality. The European Union has also had international influence on Finnish climate policy, for example through the Covenant of Mayors, which was established in 2008 and is linked to the EU's climate and energy policy (Riekkinen et al., 2020, 11–12).

The Finnish HINKU network, which Turku and Tampere are part of, provides expert assistance in promoting climate work throughout the municipalities. In the 2020 report, some municipalities confirmed the importance of this support and the availability of assistance, while others had not received the support they expected (Riekkinen et al., 2020, 42–43). In 2021, almost half of the surveyed Finnish municipalities reported that they had allocated human resources to municipalities' climate work (Puurula et al., 2022, 28). This was a significant increase from the previous survey, showing growing consideration for the issue.

In Finland in 2021, an average person produced approximately 6.8 tonnes of CO_2 emissions, whereas in Germany, the corresponding amount was 8.1 tonnes (Ritchie et al., 2020). The number has recently decreased in both countries but still remains at an unsustainable level. As Germany and Finland are industrialised countries, their emissions per GDP were also high in 2021. While in Germany the emissions were 237 tonnes of carbon dioxide equivalent per million euros of GDP, in Finland, the emissions came to 207 tonnes of carbon dioxide equivalent per million euros of GDP (UBA, 2023a).

Germany has set a goal of being greenhouse gas-neutral by 2045. By 2030, emissions are to be reduced by 65% compared to the levels of 1990. Like in Finland, a climate protection law has also been passed in Germany, which is regarded as the core of national climate policy. It contains a comprehensive climate protection programme, including a package of measures that sets out what the federal government is doing to achieve the climate protection targets. The climate protection programme operates as an overall plan for climate protection policy and lists the most important measures for transport, energy, buildings, industry, and agriculture. According to the federal government, many of the measures have already been implemented, such as the "Germany-Ticket" for public transport, the acceleration of procedures and areas for the expansion of renewable energies, and the promotion of energy-efficient construction and refurbishment of buildings (Bundesregierung, 2023).

Local climate policy in Germany is integrated into a complex multi-level system. On the one hand, cities in Germany receive regulations, incentives, and information from higher political levels; on the other hand, cities can also react to different types and options of the multi-level system (Kemmerzell & Hofmeister, 2018, 96). The topic of climate change has been part of the political debate in Germany since the 1980s. At the national level, this included the establishment of a commission on "Precautionary measures to protect the Earth's atmosphere" and a resolution by the federal government to reduce CO_2 emissions (Nagorny-Koring, 2018, 39–40). In Germany in general, the federal government is responsible for negotiating international treaties concerning climate and general regulation regarding heating and other systems, emission control, energy efficiency for new buildings, and incentive programmes for energy-related refurbishments. The state governments are responsible for contributing to the internationally and nationally agreed-upon climate goals and regulation of adjacent fields (regional planning, traffic, additional investments). The majority of the states also have their own climate protection legislation, which sets quantified and scheduled reduction targets (Roelfes, 2022).

For decades, municipalities have been committed to climate protection and have adopted their own climate protection strategies and programmes of measures. Parallel to the decisions at the federal level, reactions at the municipal level followed already in the 1990s: the so-called pioneering municipalities set their own climate targets, founded national energy agencies and are still involved in transnational city networks (e.g. Climate Alliance or Energy Cities). Around 500 German municipalities are now members of urban climate protection networks (Nagorny-Koring, 2018, 40). Thirteen German cities are even members of more than two networks. Overall, this means that more than half of Germans live in cities where local governments are involved in climate policy networks (Busch, 2015, 219). Municipalities have also institutionalised climate protection management (Roelfes, 2022). As the lowest political level in the German federal system, municipalities are responsible for climate-related local measures regarding additional restrictions for new buildings, city and traffic planning, and urban redevelopment including street and square design. As part of the recently passed law at the federal level on heat planning and the decarbonisation of heating networks, municipalities have been tasked with drawing up municipal heat planning systems. The federal government is providing financial and advisory support.

In general, each level of government is responsible for reducing its own climate emissions by green maintenance (local administration car fleets, public buildings, street lighting, urban landscaping/greening, traffic/mobility concepts, waste avoidance). Cities have their own climate plans, which do not explicitly stretch into the region. Considering that cities will be more affected than rural areas by the consequences of climate change, cities in Germany also have a key role to play regarding climate change mitigation and adaptation (Busch, 2015, 213). At the same time, cities have the potential to meet the challenges of climate change by influencing aspects such as land use planning, waste management, energy consumption, and public transport (ibid., 214).

In Germany, local authorities also play an important role in climate protection. Many local authorities have set ambitious climate targets for themselves and have established climate protection as a cross-cutting issue, which means that climate protection is fully integrated into the tasks of local government (Bulkeley & Kern, 2006; Bulkeley & Betsill, 2013). Forcing greenhouse gas neutrality in the municipal context means, for example, refurbishing the entire municipal building stock, reorganising the local transport sector and converting the energy supply to renewable energies (UBA, 2023b).

Since 2012, the Federal Ministry for the Environment has been supporting 19 municipalities and districts with the 100% Climate Protection Masterplan as part of the national climate protection initiative. The participating municipalities commit to reducing their urban greenhouse gas emissions by 95% by 2050 compared to 1990 levels and to halving their final energy consumption by 2050. A further 22 masterplan municipalities and regions joined the alliance in 2016. Since then, the state capitals of Mainz and Kiel have also joined (BMWK, 2023).

2.4 Housing Challenges Faced by Municipalities

The rising cost of housing, the incoherence of the urban structure, the lack of diverse apartments, and segregation pose major threats to housing policy in Finland (Kytö, 2013). As Antikainen et al. (2020, 5) present, there is natural regional variation in housing policy and its challenges in Finland, so there is a need to find different solutions that better acknowledge local challenges and differences in rural and urban areas. For example, the fact that Oulu has gone through a municipal merger relatively recently (2013) means that its needs as a growing central city and the needs of the smaller former municipalities must be reconciled.

The global phenomenon of rising housing prices is also visible in Finland, and it has spread to influence the middle class as well (Sutela et al., 2020, 10–11). Rents for non-subsidised housing have risen rapidly since the 2010s (Karikallio et al., 2019, 10). Turku, Tampere, and Oulu also highlight affordable housing in their housing policy documents. ARA housing, which offers affordable housing, is available in all cities, but the share of ARA-financed apartments decreased rapidly in the 2010s as the number of market-based rental apartments increased. As current inflation has hindered other construction, the production of ARA housing increased in 2023 compared to recent years (ARA, 2024, 3). However, in Finland, affordable housing is often mistakenly associated with ARA production, when in fact it is a central question of urban inequalities that concerns both lower- and middle-income households (Sutela et al., 2020, 27).

The number of people living alone has been increasing in Finland, in part due to changes in the housing allowance and the ageing baby-boomer population (Vaattovaara & Vuori, 2023, 31). The demand for smaller homes has been on the rise as a result of urbanisation (Karikallio et al., 2019, 50). The rapid increase in the number of people living alone and the demand for one-room apartments has led to drastic pressure and an increase in the construction of small apartments. In their housing policies, Turku, Tampere, and Oulu recognise not only the increase in single occupancies but also the need for a more diversified housing supply. More diverse housing could also be seen as mitigating the threat of segregation. Housing policy documents, especially in Turku and Tampere, call for a more diverse, family-suitable housing supply. This is a consequence of the tendency for families to move to surrounding municipalities because housing in the city centre is perceived as too expensive and the apartments as too small (Kytö, 2013, 18).

The problematic phenomenon of the segregation of neighbourhoods based on income, education, age structure, and/or ethnic background has become more of an issue in Finland rather recently (e.g. Rosengren et al., 2023). Finland has seen signs of increasing socioeconomic disparities in the 2000s, especially in the suburbs built in the 1960s and 1970s (Antikainen et al., 2020, 13). The evolution of segregation can be traced to the economic depression in the 1990s and how differently areas recovered economically, but it was also affected by the housing choices of highly educated residents (Rasinkangas, 2013, 241–242).

Both MAL agreements and the government-driven suburban development programme aim to establish means to increase the vitality, attractiveness, sustainability, and safety of suburbs. This is to be achieved through redensification, refurbishment, and general improvements of neighbourhood amenities. Neighbourhoods and their maintenance or refurbishment can therefore be seen as an important tool for reducing segregation (Kytö, 2013, 24). Turku, Tampere, and Oulu have successfully been part of the programme. Redensification is further emerging in all cities as a significant tool in terms of urban development and housing policy. It is justified for climate reasons, but cities also see it as an economic advantage and as a way to tackle segregation, as they hope it will diversify the housing stock and refresh the image of older suburbs (e.g. City of Tampere, 2022, 42).

Housing policy documents of all selected Finnish cities recognise the importance of housing for "special" groups such as the homeless, the elderly, and people with disabilities or severe mental health and substance abuse problems. The increasing ageing population is forcing cities to consider accessibility and versatility of housing to ensure its suitability for different ages and stages of human life (Antikainen et al., 2020, 13). The national "Housing First" programme has successfully reduced homelessness during the 2010s. Recently, the trend has been slower, and at the moment, Turku has the highest relative homelessness rate in the country (ARA, 2023, 5). The fewer homeless people there are in general, the harder the issue becomes to solve.

Climate change is accelerating at an alarming rate, and Europe is currently warming at a faster rate than any other continent (WMO, 2023). With drastic emission reductions, the pace of climate change effects can be somewhat influenced, but many effects are unavoidable and will continue for centuries (IPCC, 2023, 18). This exposes cities to the need for effective climate change adaptation rather than just mitigation. Climate change threatens not only the built environment but also people's quality of life and ability to work (Roders & Straub, 2015).

Oulu, Tampere, and Turku mostly identify similar threats and impacts of climate change. Average temperatures in Finland will rise, which will require recognising the effects and thus changing the design of housing and urban structure. The threat posed by precipitation is particularly well recognised, as snowfall in Finland will increasingly change to rainfall (Finnish Meteorological Institute, 2023). Managing floods and urban runoff will therefore be crucial, and these events will be intensified by densifying urban structure. Rising sea levels will also be a tangible threat in Oulu and Turku. Cities are widely recognising that drought, warming summers, and the urban heat island effect will bring challenges to the environment and health. Architecture and construction must create apartments that are cool in the summertime and warm enough even for mild winters. Political guidance could ensure that passive solar shading solutions are taken into account already at the designing stage. However, active solutions against the warmth and sunshine are also needed, especially during heat waves (Lahdensivu et al., 2023).

Extreme weather events, such as storms, are also mentioned as risks, although the effects of climate change are difficult to predict. Wind-driven rain is estimated to increase, which should be considered when constructing and designing housing, as it reduces the durability of buildings under certain conditions (Lahdensivu et al., 2023). Wider global impacts may also be reflected in Finland, for example in the form of climate refugees, which can raise questions of adequate housing in the future (City of Turku, 2022, 58).

These measures apply to both mitigation and adaptation, as it becomes increasingly relevant to not only build new, heat-resistant apartments but also to adapt existing ones. Adaptation is challenging, inter alia, because of the uncertainties associated with climate change (Roders & Straub, 2015, 169). The National Climate Change Adaptation Plan, which is part of Finland's Climate Change Act, obliges authorities to prepare for and adapt to climate change. Tackling this major challenge requires different levels of government and stakeholders to work together (Government of Finland, 2023b, 11). Adaptation must also take place at national, regional, and local levels (Hildén et al., 2022, 8).

In Germany, housing has been under pressure for many years. Especially in big cities, rental prices have been increasing dramatically, even when considering that wages have also increased. While this is true for metropolitan areas and smaller cities with a certain population structure (e.g. with universities, see Egner & Grabietz, 2018), it must also be acknowledged that the pattern of rising rental prices is not uniform across Germany. The three German cities all belong to the category of cities with fast-rising rental prices. The causes of this development are manifold. First, there is an imbalance between people migrating into the cities and the available housing stock. Constructing new housing is usually outpaced by natural population growth and migration from less populated areas to the cities. The latter is usually caused by a greater supply in terms of labour, education, cultural and leisure facilities, and public transport, but also other "pull factors" like general quality of life. Housing construction is restrained by limited building plots and bottlenecks in administrative processes (e.g. revision of city planning, issuing building permits), but also by real estate prices, construction material, and labour cost.

An even greater impact on rental prices was created when municipally owned housing companies sold parts of their housing stock, mostly during the 1990s. Since municipalities can directly influence the market behaviour of the housing companies they own, they can exert on the general level of rental prices in their respective city. Cities that sold their housing companies now lack the possibility of market influence. In addition, the stock of publicly subsidised apartments has decreased dramatically because there is a reduced rental price for subsidised apartments, which is fixed for a defined period of time. After the period of fixed rental prices expires, the owner of the housing unit may increase the rent or even sell the units as desired. The combined effect of less construction activity and time elapsing is that "[s]ocial housing is disappearing faster than new housing is being built" (Rink & Egner, 2022, 444).

Beyond general developments, the three German cities somewhat differ regarding their housing situations. The situation can be described as dramatic at least in two cities if we consider four parallel developments that shape the housing situation in every city: (1) the overall development in population, (2) the available housing stock, (3) rental prices, and (4) available income. What all three German cities have in common is a lack of affordable housing, caused by the co-development of the four indicators described above. While the developments are similar, they differ in size. Kiel and Mainz are quite similar; they are characterised by large universities, which cause more turnover in rental contracts, thus allowing for more rent increases by the landlords. Both cities also experience housing construction that is not keeping pace with population growth. This causes a growing gap between supply and demand in the local rental market, which again leads to increasing rents. In turn, the increment in rent is not matched by the growth in wealth. For Wiesbaden, the situation is not as dramatic as in Kiel and Mainz, but it shows that even if construction of new housing is matching population growth, the rents are still growing faster than wealth and wages.

For the average renter in the three cities, it is becoming more and more difficult to find affordable and appropriate housing. This leads to "lock-in effects", i.e. people living in single households and large apartments do not move to smaller apartments because the rental price of the new apartments may be higher than the current rent. Also, construction tends to aim at the top layers of the rental market while the lack of supply is usually for medium and cheap apartments (Prognos, 2017).

Besides the general development, there are specific problems regarding housing in the three cities. Kiel and Mainz both claim that they have limited possibilities to expand, i.e. they lack space where additional housing may be developed in larger chunks. Wiesbaden does not make the same claim but faces other problems (i.e. a hilly terrain, which increases the cost of construction for housing and the infrastructure needed, such as streets, sewage, energy provision, etc.).

In Germany, the impact of climate change is not limited to environmental challenges and extends to various societal aspects, including housing problems. The rising temperatures and changing climate patterns contribute to extreme weather events, which pose a threat to urban areas like Mainz and Wiesbaden. As temperatures continue to rise, the climate in cities like Mainz is expected to resemble that of Ancona in Italy (UBA, 2021), with potential consequences for vulnerable populations, especially the ageing generation. This poses a challenge for housing and urban planning too, as the need for climate-resilient infrastructure and housing for the elderly becomes more important. Moreover, the heightened risk of extreme weather events, such as heavy rainfall and floods, can cause damages in existing housing infrastructure and creates a demand for improved flood-resistant housing designs. The mention of forest fires (Stadt Wiesbaden, 2024) around Wiesbaden emphasises the broader environmental risks that can indirectly affect housing in these regions. In northern German cities like Kiel, rising temperatures, heavy rainfall, and sea level rise contribute to the complexity of housing challenges. Coastal cities face the additional threat of encroaching waters, necessitating strategic urban planning to address potential displacement, damaged infrastructure and instabilities in housing. The described climate change impacts cause significant implications for housing and urban planning and call for adaptive strategies to mitigate potential housing problems caused by extreme weather events and increasingly changing climatic conditions.

2.5 Connections Between Housing and Climate in Policy Documents

In the main housing and climate policy documents, the cities formulate their policy objectives, identify areas in need of action, and present measures to achieve these objectives. In Finnish documents, climate and housing are frequently connected or at least mentioned together. The connection is usually related to sustainable construction (such as wooden or low-carbon construction or refurbishment of older buildings), energy efficiency, and sustainable transport (especially public transport and cycling). Alongside these themes, the need for a more sustainable city structure through redensification arises, but each city also values the preservation of green areas and (urban) nature. Especially redensification and sustainable transport are something the cities strongly promote.

More recent documents are more inclined to connect housing and climate; for example, the newest housing policy document in Tampere (2022) strongly integrates housing and climate and offers more measurements and targets to track their actualisation. Some of these measurements include the desired level of wooden construction or of redensification. The climate documents usually cover sustainable housing, urban environment, and construction more than housing documents; for example, each of the Finnish cities' climate strategies has a section dedicated to sustainable city development, which specifically refers to a compact city structure.

In Germany, most cities have concepts or plans for climate protection. Cities like Kiel and Mainz are part of the "Masterplan Municipalities" group, which is funded by the Federal Ministry for the Environment with the National Climate Protection Initiative. These cities have the same reduction targets. However, there are also municipalities, such as Wiesbaden, that have adopted their own climate protection concept and have set their own climate protection strategy. In addition to the climate plans, some municipalities have their own housing concepts, such as Kiel and Mainz.

The plans for both climate housing establish a link to each other, so the fields are frequently connected in Germany too. The climate documents depict entire chapters on the topic of housing, such as "Climate Protection in households and residents" (Kiel), which mostly contain technical content on refurbishment projects, sustainable construction, and heat planning. A lot of attention is paid to the topic of energy efficiency in buildings. These plans also address the reduction potential in private households and in the area of urban development (Wiesbaden). In this context, the handling of new development areas, conversion areas, and topics such as redensification, urban redevelopment, and energy-efficient neighbourhood refurbishment plays a particularly important role (Wiesbaden). For example, potential savings are highlighted in this context.

As in Finland, housing is noted more in the climate documents than the topic of climate in the housing concepts. However, the housing concepts also contain statements such as "it is important to us that buildings are built in a sustainable, energy-efficient, climate-friendly way" or sections on redensification and land sealing motivated by climate policy. Nevertheless, it seems that the focus is more on the social than on the ecological aspects of housing.

All cities' climate strategies do recognise that both mitigation and adaptation should be pursued. However, the concreteness of adaptation measures and the extent of their integration into other policy programmes is another story. Advancing climate change is recognised to become costly on both economic and human capacity, and the longer it takes to become aware and manage the situation, the more costly it will become.

References

Act on Developing Housing Conditions. (1985/919 § 1). In Helsinki on 01.01.1986. Retrieved January 10, 2024, from https://www.finlex.fi/fi/laki/ajantasa/1985/19850919

Adabre, M. A., Chan, A. P. C., & Darko, A. (2022). Interactive effects of institutional, economic, social and environmental barriers on sustainable housing in a developing country. *Building and Environment, 207*, 108487. https://doi.org/10.1016/j.buildenv.2021.108487

Adamkiewicz, G., Zota, A. R., Fabian, M. P., Chahine, T., Julien, R., Spengler, J. D., & Levy, J. I. (2011). Moving environmental justice indoors: Understanding structural influences on residential exposure patterns in low-income communities. *American Journal of Public Health, 101*(S1), 238–245. https://doi.org/10.2105/AJPH.2011.300119

Alford, J., & Head, B. W. (2017). Wicked and less wicked problems: A typology and a contingency framework. *Policy & Society, 36*(3), 397–413. https://doi.org/10.1080/14494035.2017.1361634

Andelin, M., Sarasoja, A.-L., Ventovuori, T., & Junnila, S. (2015). Breaking the circle of blame for sustainable buildings – evidence from Nordic countries. *Journal of Corporate Real Estate, 17*(1), 26–45. https://doi.org/10.1108/JCRE-05-2014-0013

Antikainen, J., Pyykkönen, S., Huttunen, J., Soininvaara, I., Laakso, S., & Lönnqvist, H. (2020). *Kaupunkiseutujen ja kuntien asuntopoliittisten ohjelmien arviointi ja kehittäminen [The evaluation and development of housing policy programmes of city regions and municipalities].* Loppuraportti. MAL-verkosto ja asumisen rahoitus- ja kehittämiskeskus ARA. Retrieved December 12, 2023, from https://mal-verkosto.fi/wp-content/uploads/2020/05/Liite-1.-Kaupunkiseutujen-ja-kuntien-asuntopoliittisten-ohjelmien-arviointi-ja-kehitta%CC%88minen-loppuraportti-MDI-1.pdf

ARA. (2023). *Asunnottomat 2022 [The homeless in 2022].* Selvitys 2/2023. Asumisen rahoitus- ja kehittämiskeskus (ARA). Retrieved December 18, 2024, from https://ysaatio.fi/wp-content/uploads/2023/08/Asunnottomat_2022-3.pdf

ARA. (2024). *Ara-tuotanto 2023 [ARA production in 2023].* Selvitys 1/2024. Asumisen rahoitus- ja kehittämiskeskus (ARA). Retrieved December 18, 2024, from https://www.ara.fi/fi/document/ara-tuotanto-2023-0

Artmann, M., Inostroza, L., & Fan, P. (2019). Urban sprawl, compact urban development and green cities. How much do we know, how much do we agree? *Ecological Indicators, 96*(2), 3–9. https://doi.org/10.1016/j.ecolind.2018.10.059

Berardi, U. (2013). Stakeholders' influence on the adoption of energy-saving technologies in Italian homes. *Energy Policy, 60,* 520–530. https://doi.org/10.1016/j.enpol.2013.04.074

Bibri, S. E., & Krogstie, J. (2020). Smart eco-city strategies and solutions for sustainability: The cases of Royal Seaport, Stockholm, and Western Harbor, Malmö, Sweden. *Urban Science, 4*(1), 11. https://doi.org/10.3390/urbansci4010011

Bramley, G., & Power, S. (2009). Urban form and social sustainability: The role of density and housing type. *Environment and Planning. B, Planning & Design, 36*(1), 30–48. https://doi.org/10.1068/b33129

Bulkeley, H., & Betsill, M. M. (2013). Revisiting the urban politics of climate change. *Environmental Politics, 22*(1), 136–154. https://doi.org/10.1080/09644016.2013.755797

Bulkeley, H., & Kern, K. (2006). Local government and the governing of climate change in Germany and the UK. *Urban Studies, 43*(12), 2237–2259. https://doi.org/10.1080/00420980600936491

BMWK – Bundesministerium für Wirtschaft und Klimaschutz [Federal Ministry for Economic Affairs and Climate Protection]. (2023). *Masterplan 100% Klimaschutz. Förderung von Kommunen in Masterplan-Kommunen [Masterplan 100% climate protection. Promotion of municipalities in masterplan municipalities].* Retrieved December 14, 2023, from https://www.klimaschutz.de/de/foerderung/foerderprogramme/masterplan-100-klimaschutz

Bundesregierung [German Federal Government]. (2021). *Koalitionsvertrag. [Coalition Agreement].* Retrieved December 8, 2023, from https://www.bundesregierung.de/breg-de/service/gesetzesvorhaben/koalitionsvertrag-2021-1990800

Bundesregierung [German Federal Government]. (2023). *Klimaschutzgesetz und Klimaschutzprogramm. [Climate Protection Act and Climate Protection Programme].* Retrieved December 14, 2023, from https://www.bundesregierung.de/breg-de/themen/tipps-fuer-verbraucher/klimaschutzgesetz-2197410

Busch, H. (2015). Linked for action? An analysis of transnational municipal climate networks in Germany. *International Journal of Urban Sustainable Development, 7*(2), 213–231. https://doi.org/10.1080/19463138.2015.1057144

Callewaert, J. (2002). The importance of local history for understanding and addressing environmental injustice. *Local Environment, 7*(3), 257–267.

City of Tampere. (2022). *Tampereen kaupungin asunto- ja maapolitiikan linjaukset 2022–2025 [The housing and land policy guidelines of City of Tampere 2022–2025].* Retrieved December 11, 2024, from https://www.tampere.fi/sites/default/files/2022-09/Tampereen%20kaupungin%20asunto-%20ja%20maapolitiikan%20linjaukset%202022-2025_web%20%281%29_0.pdf

City of Turku. (2022). *Ilmastosuunnitelma 2029 - Turun kaupungin kestävä ilmasto- ja energiatoimintasuunnitelma 2029 [The Climate Programme 2029 – The Sustainable Climate and Energy Action Plan of City of Turku].* 2/2022. Retrieved March 6, 2024, from https://issuu.com/turunviestinta/docs/turun_ilmastosuunnitelma_2029

References

Crabtree, L., & Hes, D. (2009). Sustainability uptake in housing in metropolitan Australia: An institutional problem, not a technological one. *Housing Studies, 24*(2), 203–224. https://doi.org/10.1080/02673030802704337

Chiu, R. L. (2004). Socio-cultural sustainability of housing: A conceptual exploration. *Housing, Theory and Society, 21*(2), 65–76. https://doi.org/10.1080/14036090410014999

de Wilde, P., Rafiq, Y., & Beck, M. (2008). Uncertainties in predicting the impact of climate change on thermal performance of domestic buildings in the UK. *Building Services Engineering Research & Technology, 29*(1), 7–26. https://doi.org/10.1177/0143624407087261

Difu – Deutsches Institut für Urbanistik [German Institute of Urban Affairs]. (2022). *OB-Barometer [Mayors' survey] 2022*. Retrieved November 12, 2024, from https://difu.de/0ddac9b623c5419 9d298da142c41e71596a5f65c/5f4ba4a0-729b- 9b5e-c13ca8687ca1169d/tap2_3CQyYi_dec/OB-Barometer2022_online.pdf

Dobes, L. (2008). Getting real about adapting to climate change: using 'real options' to address the uncertainties. *Agenda (Canberra, Australia), 15*(3), 55–69. https://doi.org/10.22459/AG.15.03.2008.04

EEA (European Environment Agency). (2024). *Renewable Energy*. Retrieved October 22, 2024, from https://www.eea.europa.eu/en/topics/in-depth/renewable-energy

Egner, B. (2023). Sustainability of housing in times of crisis. *PoWiNE Working Paper-Magdeburger politikwissenschaftliche Beiträge zu Nachhaltigkeit in Forschung und Lehre, 3*, 14–19. https://doi.org/10.24352/UB.OVGU-2023-004

Egner, B., & Grabietz, K. J. (2018). In search of determinants for quoted housing rents: Empirical evidence from major German cities. *Urban Research & Practice, 11*(4), 460–477. https://doi.org/10.1080/17535069.2017.1395906

Egner, B., Kayser, M. A., Böhler, H., & Grabietz, K. J. (2018). *Lokale Wohnungspolitik in Deutschland [Local housing policy in Germany]*. Working Paper Forschungsförderung, 100, Hans-Böckler-Stiftung, Düsseldorf. Retrieved February 26, 2024, from https://www.econstor.eu/bitstream/10419/216025/1/hbs-fofoe-wp-100-2018.pdf

Finnish Meteorological Institute. (2023). *Näin ilmastonmuutos näkyy Suomessa [How climate change is visible in Finland]*. Retrieved December 8, 2023, from https://www.ilmatieteenlaitos.fi/uutinen/5KaRzesbqBjKp1MocorJIy

Finnish Ministry of the Environment. (2022a). *Kohti hiilineutraalia Suomea – hallitus hyväksyi keskipitkän aikavälin ilmastopolitiikan suunnitelman [Towards a carbon-neutral Finland - The government accepted the medium length climate policy plan]*. Retrieved December 8, 2023, from https://ym.fi/-/kohti-hiilineutraalia-suomea-hallitus-hyvaksyi-keskipitkan-aikavalin-ilmastopolitiikan-suunnitelman

Finnish Ministry of the Environment. (2022b). *Ilmastovuosikertomus 2022, tiivistelmä [Annual Climate Report 2022, Summary]*. Helsinki. Retrieved December 8, 2023, from https://julkaisut.valtioneuvosto.fi/bitstream/handle/10024/164392/YM-ilmastovuosikertomus-tiivistelm%c3%a4_2022_220912_verkkoon.pdf?sequence=2&isAllowed=y

Finnish Ministry of the Environment. (2022c). *Keskipitkän aikavälin ilmastopolitiikan suunnitelma – Kohti hiilineutraalia yhteiskuntaa 2035 [Medium length climate policy plan – Towards a carbon neutral society 2035]*. Ympäristöministeriön julkaisuja 2022:12. Finnish Ministry of the Environment. Retrieved December 8, 2023, from https://julkaisut.valtioneuvosto.fi/bitstream/handle/10024/164186/YM_2022_12.pdf?sequence=4

Finnish Ministry of the Environment. (2023a). *Rakentamislaki ohjaa kestävää rakentamista. [The Building Act guides sustainable construction]*. Retrieved January 8, 2024, from https://ym.fi/rakentamislaki

Finnish Ministry of the Environment. (2023b). *Suomen kansallinen ilmastopolitiikka [The National Climate Policy of Finland]*. Retrieved January 8, 2024, from https://ym.fi/suomen-kansallinen-ilmastopolitiikka

Gluch, P., Gustafsson, M., Thuvander, L., & Baumann, H. (2014). Charting corporate greening: Environmental management trends in Sweden. *Building Research and Information: The International Journal of Research, Development and Demonstration, 42*(3), 318–329. https://doi.org/10.1080/09613218.2014.855873

Government of Finland. (2021). *Asuntopoliittinen kehittämisohjelma vuosiksi 2021–2018 [Housing Policy Development Programme for 2021–2018]*. Valtioneuvoston selonteko. Retrieved December 8, 2023, from https://www.eduskunta.fi/FI/vaski/JulkaisuMetatieto/Documents/VNS_12+2021.pdf

Government of Finland. (2023a). *Vahva ja välittävä Suomi – Pääministeri Petteri Orpon hallituksen ohjelma 20.6.2023 [A strong and committed Finland: Programme of Prime Minister Petteri Orpo's Government 20 June 2023]*. Valtioneuvoston julkaisuja 2023:58. Valtioneuvosto. Retrieved December 8, 2023, from https://julkaisut.valtioneuvosto.fi/bitstream/handle/10024/165042/Paaministeri-Petteri-Orpon-hallituksen-ohjelma-20062023.pdf?sequence=1&isAllowed=y

Government of Finland. (2023b). *Valtioneuvoston selonteko kansallisesta ilmastonmuutokseen sopeutumissuunnitelmasta vuoteen 2030 [Government of Finland's Report of National Climate Change Adaptation Plan 2030]*. Valtioneuvoston julkaisuja 2023:73. Valtioneuvosto. Retrieved December 8, 2023, from https://julkaisut.valtioneuvosto.fi/bitstream/handle/10024/165337/VN_2023_73.pdf?sequence=1&isAllowed=y

Granath Hansson, A. (2020). Meeting a growing homelessness: How could three Swedish affordable housing initiatives be analysed from perspectives of social and economic sustainability? *Nordic Journal of Surveying and Real Estate Research, 15*(1), 7. https://doi.org/10.30672/nisr.75140

Hagbert, P., & Femenías, P. (2016). Sustainable homes, or simply energy-efficient buildings? *Journal of Housing and the Built Environment, 31*(1), 1–17. https://doi.org/10.1007/s10901-015-9440-y

Hayles, C. S., & Dean, M. (2015). Social housing tenants, climate change and sustainable living: A study of awareness, behaviours and willingness to adapt. *Sustainable Cities and Society, 17*, 35–45. https://doi.org/10.1016/j.scs.2015.03.007

Hayles, C., Huddleston, M., Chinowsky, P., & Helman, J. (2022). Quantifying the effects of projected climate change on the durability and service life of housing in Wales, UK. *Buildings (Basel), 12*(2), 184. https://doi.org/10.3390/buildings12020184

Head, B. W. (2019). Forty years of wicked problems literature: Forging closer links to policy studies. *Policy & Society, 38*(2), 180–197. https://doi.org/10.1080/14494035.2018.1488797

Head, B. W., & Alford, J. (2015). Wicked problems: Implications for public policy and management. *Administration & Society, 47*(6), 711–739.

Herath, S., Cilliers, E. J., & Mussi, E. (2024). A triple whammy: How urban heat, housing unaffordability and disadvantage affect urban spatial resilience. *Frontiers in Sustainable Cities, 6*. https://doi.org/10.3389/frsc.2024.1244187

Herazo, B., & Lizarralde, G. (2016). Understanding stakeholders' approaches to sustainability in building projects. *Sustainable Cities and Society, 26*, 240–254. https://doi.org/10.1016/j.scs.2016.05.019

Hildén, M., Tikkakoski, P., Sorvali, J., Mettiäinen, I., Käyhkö, J., Helminen, M., Määttä, H., Berninger, K., Meriläinen, P., Ahonen, S., Kolstela, J., Juhola, S., Tynkkynen, O., Gregow, H., Groundstroem, F., Halonen, J. I., Munck af Rosenschöld, J., Tuomenvirta, H., Carter, T., Lehtonen, H., Luomaranta, A., & Mäkelä, A. (2022). *Ilmastonmuutokseen sopeutuminen Suomessa – nykytila ja kehitysnäkymät [Adaptation to climate change in Finland – The current state and development outlooks]*. Valtioneuvoston selvitys- ja tutkimustoiminnan julkaisusarja 2022:55. Valtioneuvosto. Retrieved December 8, 2023, from https://julkaisut.valtioneuvosto.fi/bitstream/handle/10024/164300/VNTEAS_2022_55.pdf?sequence=1&isAllowed=y

IPCC. (2023). Summary for policymakers. In H. Lee & J. Romero (Eds.), *Climate Change 2023: Synthesis Report* (pp. 1–34). Contribution of Working Groups I, II and III to the Sixth Assessment Report of the Intergovernmental Panel on Climate Change. IPCC. https://doi.org/10.59327/IPCC/AR6-9789291691647.001

Jonsson, O., Frögren, J., Haak, M., Slaug, B., & Iwarsson, S. (2021). Understanding the wicked problem of providing accessible housing for the ageing population in Sweden. *International

Journal of Environmental Research and Public Health, 18(3), 1–21. https://doi.org/10.3390/ijerph18031169

Karikallio, H., Keskinen, P., Kiviholma, S., Reijonen, H., Ruuskanen, O., Vuori, L., Härmälä, V., & Lamminkoski, H. (2019). *Pienten asuntojen osuus asuntotuotannossa ja vaikutukset asuinalueiden eriytymiseen* [*The amount of small apartments in housing production and the effects on residential segregation*]. PTT-raportteja 262. Pellervon taloustutkimus PTT. Retrieved December 12, 2023, from https://www.ptt.fi/wp-content/uploads/media/pttrap262.pdf

Kemmerzell, J., & Hofmeister, A. (2018). Innovationen in der Klimapolitik deutscher Großstädte. Der Einfluss überlokalen Handelns im Vergleich [Innovations in the climate policy of major German cities. A comparison of the influence of supra-local action]. *Politische Vierteljahresschrift, 60*, 95–126. https://doi.org/10.1007/s11615-018-0134-4

Kettl, D. (2009). *The next government of the United States: Why our institutions fail us and how to fix them*. W.W. Norton.

Krapp, M. C., Vaché, M., Egner, B., Schulze, K., & Thomas, S. (2021). *Housing policies in the European Union. Annex: Country Reports*. Institut Wohnen und Umwelt GmbH.

Krummacher, M. (2011). Kommunale Wohnungspolitik [Local housing policy]. In H.-J. Dahme & N. Wohlfahrt (Eds.), *Handbuch Kommunale Sozialpolitik* (pp. 201–214). VS Verlag für Sozialwissenschaften.

Kuntaliitto. (2015). *Asuntopoliittiset linjaukset* [*Housing policy guidelines*]. Retrieved December 8, 2023, from https://www.kuntaliitto.fi/sites/default/files/media/file/1Kuntaliiton%20asuntopoliittiset%20linjaukset.pdf

Kytö, H. (2013). Asumisen uhkakuvat ja muutokset [*Threats and changes of housing*]. *Tieteessä tapahtuu, 31*, 18–24. Tieteellisten seurain valtuuskunta. Retrieved December 8, 2023, from https://journal.fi/tt/article/view/8990/6545

Lahdensivu, J., Pakkala, T., Pikkuvirta, J., Räsänen, A., Alastalo, S., Karvonen, A., Täubel, M., Pekkanen, J., Juntunen, M., Farahani, A. V., Jokisalo, J., Kosonen, R., Jylhä, K., Lanki, T., Leino, O., & Kollanus, V. (2023). *Rakennusten kosteusvauriot ja ylilämpeneminen muuttuvassa ilmastossa – RAIL* [*Water damage and overheating in the changing climate – RAIL*]. Valtioneuvoston selvitys- ja tutkimustoiminnan julkaisusarja 2023:2. Valtioneuvosto. Retrieved March 12, 2024, from https://julkaisut.valtioneuvosto.fi/bitstream/handle/10024/164539/VN_TEAS_2023_2.pdf?sequence=1&isAllowed=y

Lawrence, R. J. (2017). Constancy and change: Key issues in housing and health research, 1987–2017. *International Journal of Environmental Research and Public Health, 14*, 763. https://doi.org/10.3390/ijerph14070763

Levin, K., Cashore, B., Bernstein, S., & Auld, G. (2012). Overcoming the tragedy of super wicked problems: Constraining our future selves to ameliorate global climate change. *Policy Sciences, 45*(2), 123–152. https://doi.org/10.1007/s11077-012-9151-0

Lima, V. (2021). From housing crisis to housing justice: Towards a radical right to a home. *Urban Studies, 58*(16), 3282–3298.

Lovell, H. (2004). Framing sustainable housing as a solution to climate change. *Journal of Environmental Policy & Planning, 6*(1), 35–55. https://doi.org/10.1080/1523908042000259677

Lönngren, J., & Van Poeck, K. (2021). Wicked problems: A mapping review of the literature. *International Journal of Sustainable Development & World Ecology, 28*(6), 481–502. https://doi.org/10.1080/13504509.2020.1859415

Maalsen, S. (2020). Revising the smart home as assemblage. *Housing Studies, 35*(9), 1534–1549. https://doi.org/10.1080/02673037.2019.1655531

Marchesi, M., Tweed, C., & Gerber, D. (2020). Applying circular economy principles to urban housing. *IOP Conference Series. Earth and Environmental Science, 588*(5), 52065. https://doi.org/10.1088/1755-1315/588/5/052065

Mariano, C., & Marino, M. (2023). The climate-proof planning towards the ecological transition: Isola Sacra—Fiumicino (Italy) between flood risk and urban development prospectives. *Sustainability, 15*(10), 8387. https://doi.org/10.3390/su15108387

Martinez, M. (2020). *Squatters in the capitalist city: Housing, justice, and urban politics.* Taylor & Francis.

Martiskainen, M., & Kivimaa, P. (2018). Creating innovative zero carbon homes in the United Kingdom — Intermediaries and champions in building projects. *Environmental Innovation and Societal Transitions, 26,* 15–31. https://doi.org/10.1016/j.eist.2017.08.002

McKinlay, A., Baldwin, C., & Stevens, N. J. (2019). Size matters: Dwelling size as a critical factor for sustainable urban development. *Urban Policy and Research, 37*(2), 135–150. https://doi.org/10.1080/08111146.2017.1374944

Minixhofer, P., Scharf, B., Hafner, S., Weiss, O., Henöckl, C., Greiner, M., Room, T., & Stangl, R. (2022). Towards the circular soil concept: Optimization of engineered soils for green infrastructure application. *Sustainability, 14,* 905. https://doi.org/10.3390/su14020905

Moore, T., & Doyon, A. (2023). *A transition to sustainable housing: Progress and prospects for a low carbon housing future* (1st ed.). Springer Nature Singapore. https://doi.org/10.1007/978-981-99-2760-9

Moser, S. C. (2010). Communicating climate change: History, challenges, process and future directions. *Wiley Interdisciplinary Reviews. Climate Change, 1*(1), 31–53. https://doi.org/10.1002/wcc.11

Mulliner, E., Smallbone, K., & Maliene, V. (2013). An assessment of sustainable housing affordability using a multiple criteria decision making method. *Omega (Oxford), 41*(2), 270–279. https://doi.org/10.1016/j.omega.2012.05.002

Nagorny-Koring, N. (2018). *Kommunen im Klimawandel. Best practices als chance zur grünen transformation? [Municipalities in a changing climate. Best practices as an opportunity for green transformation?]* (1st ed.). Transcript Publishing.

Noordegraaf, M., Douglas, S., Geuijen, K., & Van Der Steen, M. (2019). Weaknesses of wickedness: A critical perspective on wickedness theory. *Policy & Society, 38*(2), 278–297.

Peters, B. G. (2017). What is so wicked about wicked problems? A conceptual analysis and a research program. *Policy & Society, 36*(3), 385–396. https://doi.org/10.1080/14494035.2017.1361633

Peters, B. G., & Tarpey, M. (2019). Are wicked problems really so wicked? Perceptions of policy problems. *Policy & Society, 38*(2), 218–236. https://doi.org/10.1080/14494035.2019.1626595

Power, A. (2010). Housing and sustainability: Demolition or refurbishment? *Proceedings of the Institution of Civil Engineers. Urban design and planning, 163*(4), 205–216. https://doi.org/10.1680/udap.2010.163.4.205

Prognos. (2017). *Wohnraumbedarf in Deutschland und den regionalen Wohnungsmärkten. Endbericht. [Housing demand in Germany and the regional housing markets. Final report].* Prognos.

Puurula, J., Hildén, M., Sorvali, J., & Jalonen, P. (2022). *Kuntien ja maakuntien ilmastotyön tilanne 2021 [The situation of municipal and regional climate work in 2021].* Suomen Kuntaliitto.

Rasinkangas, J. (2013). *Sosiaalinen eriytyminen Turun kaupunkiseudulla - Tutkimus asumisen alueellisista muutoksista ja asumispreferensseistä [Social segregation in Turku City Region - A research on regional changes of housing and housing preferences].* Tutkimuksia A 43. Siirtolaisinstituutti. Retrieved December 8, 2023, from https://www.doria.fi/bitstream/handle/10024/178457/A-43%20ISBN%20978-952-5889-50-5%20Jarkko%20Rasinkangas%20-%20Sosiaalinen%20eriytyminen%20Turun%20kaupunkiseudulla.pdf?sequence=1&isAllowed=y

Richter, J. (2023). German housing policy and the current state of the housing market in Germany. *Sociedade e Território, 35*(1), 73–88.

Riekkinen, V., Saikku, L., Karhinen, S., Aro, R., Helonheimo, T., Peltomaa, J., Pitkänen, K., Lounasheimo, J., Kokkonen, V., & Seppälä, J. (2020). *Kohti hiilineutraalia kuntaa: ilmastoverkoston vaikutus kunnan ilmastotyöhön ja päästöihin [Towards a carbon neutral municipality: The effect of climate network in municipal climate work and emissions].* Suomen ympäristökeskuksen raportteja 20. SYKE. Retrieved December 8, 2023, from https://helda.helsinki.fi/server/api/core/bitstreams/6c39f87f-fada-4559-ae1b-c60740c4b8a6/content

Rink, D., & Egner, B. (2020). Lokale Wohnungspolitik: Agenda, Diskurs, Forschungsstand. [Local housing policy: Agenda, discourse, state of research]. In D. Rink & B. Egner (Eds.), *Lokale Wohnungspolitik. Beispiele aus deutschen Städten* (pp. 9–42). Nomos.

Rink, D., & Egner, B. (2022). Local housing markets and local housing policies: A comparative analysis of 14 German cities. *International Journal of Housing Policy, 22*(3), 430–450.

Ritchey, T. (2013). Wicked problems. *Acta Morphologica Generalis, 2*(1).

Ritchie, H., Roser, M., & Rosado, P. (2020). *CO_2 and greenhouse gas emissions.* OurWorldInData.org. Retrieved February 20, 2024, from https://ourworldindata.org/co2-and-greenhouse-gas-emissions

Rittel, H. W., & Webber, M. M. (1973). Dilemmas in a general theory of planning. *Policy Sciences, 4*(2), 155–169.

Roders, M., & Straub, A. (2015). Assessment of the likelihood of implementation strategies for climate change adaptation measures in Dutch social housing. *Building and Environment, 83*, 168–176. https://doi.org/10.1016/j.buildenv.2014.07.014

Roelfes, M. (2022). *Klimapolitik in Deutschland.* [Climate politics in Germany]. *Bundeszentrale für politische Bildung.* [*Federal Agency for Civic Education*]. Retrieved December 14, 2023, from https://www.bpb.de/themen/klimawandel/dossier-klimawandel/509727/klimapolitik-in-deutschland/#node-content-title-1

Rosengren, K., Rasinkangas, J., & Ruonavaara, H. (2023). Awareness of segregation in a welfare state: A Finnish local policy perspective. *Housing Studies*, 1–22.

Rubaszek, J., Szymanowski, M., Michalski, A., Tatko, R., & Weber-Siwirska, M. (2021). Procedure for the selection and evaluation of prefabricated housing buildings for the implementation of green roofs in the context of Urban Heat Island mitigation. The example of Wrocław, Poland. *PLoS One, 16*(10), e0258641. https://doi.org/10.1371/journal.pone.0258641

Schramm, L. (2024). Some differences, many similarities: Comparing Europe's responses to the 1973 oil crisis and the 2022 gas crisis. *European Political Science Review*, 1–16.

Seppälä, J., Saikku, L., Soimakallio, S., Lounasheimo, J., Regina, K., & Ollikainen, M. (2019). *Hiilineutraalius ilmastopolitiikassa – Valtiot, alueet ja kunnat* [*Carbon neutrality in climate policy – States, regions and municipalities*]. Suomen ilmastopaneelin raportti 5a/2019. Retrieved December 8, 2023, from https://ilmastopaneeli.fi/hae-julkaisuja/hiilineutraalius-ilmastopolitiikassa-valtiot-alueet-ja-kunnat/

Sev, A. (2009). How can the construction industry contribute to sustainable development? A conceptual framework. *Sustainable Development (Bradford, West Yorkshire, England), 17*(3), 161–173. https://doi.org/10.1002/sd.373

Seyfang, G. (2010). Community action for sustainable housing: Building a low-carbon future. *Energy Policy, 38*(12), 7624–7633. https://doi.org/10.1016/j.enpol.2009.10.027

Sharifi, A. (2020). Trade-offs and conflicts between urban climate change mitigation and adaptation measures: A literature review. *Journal of Cleaner Production, 276*, 122813. https://doi.org/10.1016/j.jclepro.2020.122813

Smets, P., & van Lindert, P. (2016). Sustainable housing and the urban poor. *International Journal of Urban Sustainable Development, 8*(1), 1–9. https://doi.org/10.1080/19463138.2016.1168825

Sovacool, B. K., Lipson, M. M., & Chard, R. (2019). Temporality, vulnerability, and energy justice in household low carbon innovations. *Energy Policy, 128*, 495–504. https://doi.org/10.1016/j.enpol.2019.01.010

Stadt Wiesbaden. (2024). *Waldbrandgefahr.* https://www.wiesbaden.de/leben-in-wiesbaden/freizeit/natur-erleben/stadtwald/Waldbrandgefahr.php

Storbjörk, S., & Hjerpe, M. (2022). Stuck in experimentation: Exploring practical experiences and challenges of using floating housing to climate-proof waterfront urban development in Sweden. *Journal of Housing and the Built Environment, 37*(4), 2263–2284. https://doi.org/10.1007/s10901-022-09942-4

Storbjörk, S., Hjerpe, M., & Glaas, E. (2019). Using public-private interplay to climate-proof urban planning? Critical lessons from developing a new housing district in Karlstad, Sweden.

Journal of Environmental Planning and Management, 62(4), 568–585. https://doi.org/10.108 0/09640568.2018.1434490

Sutela, E., Ruoppila, S., Rasinkangas, J., & Juvenius, J. (2020). Kohtuuhintaisen asumisen hajanainen kokonaisuus [The scattered big picture of affordable housing]. *Yhdyskuntasuunnittelu, 58*(1), 10–32. https://doi.org/10.33357/ys.89282

Syed Jamaludin, S. Z. H., Hamid, S. H. A., & Mohd Noor, S. N. A. (2020). Assessing the challenges of integration affordable and sustainable housing from economic perspectives. *IOP Conference Series. Earth and Environmental Science, 498*(1). https://doi.org/10.1088/1755-1315/498/1/012089

Takano, A., Hughes, M., & Winter, S. (2014). A multidisciplinary approach to sustainable building material selection: A case study in a Finnish context. *Building and Environment, 82*, 526–535. https://doi.org/10.1016/j.buildenv.2014.09.026

Tayefi Nasrabadi, M., Larimian, T., Timmis, A., & Yigitcanlar, T. (2024). Mapping four decades of housing inequality research: Trends, insights, knowledge gaps, and research directions. *Sustainable Cities and Society, 113*, 105693. https://doi.org/10.1016/j.scs.2024.105693

Taylor, C., Roy, K., Dani, A. A., Lim, J. B. P., De Silva, K., & Jones, M. (2023). Delivering sustainable housing through material choice. *Sustainability, 15*(4), 3331. https://doi.org/10.3390/su15043331

Termeer, C. J., Dewulf, A., Breeman, G., & Stiller, S. J. (2015). Governance capabilities for dealing wisely with wicked problems. *Administration & Society, 47*(6), 680–710. https://doi.org/10.1177/0095399712469195

Turnbull, N., & Hoppe, R. (2019). Problematizing 'wickedness': A critique of the wicked problems concept, from philosophy to practice. *Policy & Society, 38*(2), 315–337. https://doi.org/1 0.1080/14494035.2018.1488796

UBA – Umweltbundesamt. [Federal Environment Agency]. (2021). *Klimatische Zwillingsstädte in Europa*. Retrieved December 20, 2023, from https://www.umweltbundesamt.de/klimatische-zwillingsstaedte-in-europa#herausforderung-fur-okosysteme-menschen-stadte-und-regionen

UBA – Umweltbundesamt. [Federal Environment Agency]. (2023a). *Treibhausgas-Emissionen in der Europäischen Union*. [*Greenhouse gas emissions in the European Union*]. Retrieved December 14, 2023, from https://www.umweltbundesamt.de/daten/klima/treibhausgas-emissionen-in-der-europaeischen-union#hauptverursache

UBA – Umweltbundesamt. [Federal Environment Agency]. (2023b). *Kommunaler Klimaschutz*. [*Municipal climate protection*]. Retrieved December 14, 2023, from https://www.umweltbundesamt.de/themen/klima-energie/klimaschutz-energiepolitik-in-deutschland/kommunaler-klimaschutz#Rolle

Vaattovaara, M., & Vuori, P. (2023). *Asuntorakentamisen muutokset pääkaupunkiseudulla ja Tampereella vuosina 2015–2021* [*The changes in housing construction in Helsinki Metropolitan Area and Tampere in 2015–2021*]. Tutkimuskatsauksia 2023:2. Helsingin kaupunginkanslia. Retrieved December 12, 2024, from https://kaupunkitieto.hel.fi/sites/default/files/23_06_01_Tutkimuskatsauksia_2_0.pdf

Wang, J., Dane, G. Z., & Timmermans, H. J. P. (2021). Carsharing-facilitating neighbourhood choice: A mixed logit model. *Journal of Housing and the Built Environment, 36*(3), 1033–1054. https://doi.org/10.1007/s10901-020-09791-z

WCED. (1987). *Report of the World Commission on Environment and Development: Our common future*. United Nations.

Willand, N., & Horne, R. (2018). "They are grinding us into the ground" – The lived experience of (in)energy justice amongst low-income older households. *Applied Energy, 226*, 61–70. https://doi.org/10.1016/j.apenergy.2018.05.079

Winston, N. (2014). Sustainable communities? A comparative perspective on urban housing in the European Union. *European Planning Studies, 22*(7), 1384–1406. https://doi.org/10.108 0/09654313.2013.788612

References

Winston, N. (2022). Sustainable community development: Integrating social and environmental sustainability for sustainable housing and communities. *Sustainable Development (Bradford, West Yorkshire, England), 30*(1), 191–202. https://doi.org/10.1002/sd.2238

Winston, N., & Eastaway, M. P. (2008). Sustainable housing in the urban context: International sustainable development indicator sets and housing. *Social Indicators Research, 87*(2), 211–221. https://doi.org/10.1007/s11205-007-9165-8

WMO. (2023). *State of the Climate in Europe 2022*. WMO-No. 1320. World Meteorological Organization. Retrieved December 8, 2023, from https://community.wmo.int/en/news/wmos-state-climate-europe-report-2022-urges-immediate-action-europes-climate-crisis

Open Access This chapter is licensed under the terms of the Creative Commons Attribution 4.0 International License (http://creativecommons.org/licenses/by/4.0/), which permits use, sharing, adaptation, distribution and reproduction in any medium or format, as long as you give appropriate credit to the original author(s) and the source, provide a link to the Creative Commons license and indicate if changes were made.

The images or other third party material in this chapter are included in the chapter's Creative Commons license, unless indicated otherwise in a credit line to the material. If material is not included in the chapter's Creative Commons license and your intended use is not permitted by statutory regulation or exceeds the permitted use, you will need to obtain permission directly from the copyright holder.

Chapter 3
Councillors' Views on Housing and Climate

Most interviewees recognise the link between housing and climate change, although it tends to come up in interviews only when asked directly. The interviewees show awareness that housing produces a significant number of emissions, and they consider climate change to "absolutely be taken into account in housing policy" (O9). Yet, the climate perspective is by no means the only perspective of housing and can often be overshadowed by other prioritised perspectives. In Finland, most interviewees currently perceive the intersection of housing and climate to be strong. However, some feel that the link could be stronger, or they question how to account for climate more and less in housing—and from their perspective, it is easier to slip into the "less" side.

This chapter first discusses the power of the municipalities and councillors. It then explains how councillors in both Finland and Germany see the integration of climate and housing in construction, technological measures, and energy. The connections continue in the form of housing location and environment, as councillors reflect on a compact but green urban structure. The chapter concludes with a section on the future and how little the councillors consider it in the interviews.

3.1 Municipal Policy and Priorities

Policymakers in both countries recognise that housing sustainability is influenced by national legislation and regulation as well as international arrangements—and that they oblige things forward. They also acknowledge that the cities have ambitious climate policies, and in Finland, these have led to stricter criteria of emissions from construction and housing. However, many Finnish interviewees recognise that there is a lack of systematic calculation of emissions during construction, and politicians are forced to make compromises (Ta1, Ta8, Ta9, Tu4, Tu5, Tu7, O8, O10). Climate change mitigation is perceived to be "always present" in decision-making and strategies, but the question is, of course, how *much* climate change is considered

(O8, Ta8, Tu10): "You can pay more or less attention to [climate change in construction], and of course most of the time it's not given enough attention" (O8). Some councillors express a strong sense of responsibility as decision-makers to strive for the most ecological future possible (O3, O4).

Lack of full consensus on climate targets or how to achieve housing policy guidelines poses challenges in municipal policy. The relationship between the more progressive left-wing and more conservative right-wing parties in the council is described as a tennis match where issues such as climate and the economy or private motoring and public transport are easily pitted against each other (O1, O6, Tu6). Questions are raised about how much climate change mitigation is allowed to cost (O2) or how much responsibility Finns should have in terms of global emissions (O10). Climate change is also perceived as an ideological issue (Ta1, Ta2, Ta7, O4): "Climate issues in politics are very—tense. It may be opposed just for the joy of opposing" (Ta1). This description applies to Germany as well, where there is talk of "ideological things" or "ideological discussions" (Mz2, Mz4, K6), which are led by the liberals in Germany. In this context, one person perceives the administration of the City of Kiel as very "lecturing and advertising" about energy and climate issues. But regarding the climate-related desolate state of its municipal buildings, the reaction to this was "before the administration wants to educate the citizens, it should first clean up its own backyard" (K6).

A problem highlighted by Finnish interviewees is the "conservative construction industry", which is seen as unwilling to invest in ecological sustainability (Tu2, Ta1, Ta4, Ta8, Ta9). Some see that the construction sector needs a "kick-start" towards more sustainable solutions, which could be achieved through different incentives or restrictions, such as state subsidies, taxation, conditions for the transfer of land or land allocation competitions (Ta1, Ta4, Ta6, Ta8, Ta9, Tu4, Tu6, Tu7, Tu10 O1, O4, O7, O8, O10). In contrast, private foundations are perceived as innovative and proactive in the pursuit of environmental sustainability (Ta1, Tu6, Tu7, Ta8, Ta9): "These rental housing projects, foundations in particular, are not profit-making, so they have a completely different approach, they want to try new things, they perhaps genuinely want to think about climate issues" (Ta1).

Finnish councillors recognise their power over the city's development. Some believe that this power should be used to guide construction more (Tu5, O5, O8), while others see that the market can be trusted to solve sustainability issues in the construction sector (O1, Tu6). However, some perceive councillors as having relatively little involvement or power in construction (Tu2, O5): "As a decision-maker, I can't be entirely sure how the construction is executed. I don't have the expertise either, and even if I did, I wouldn't go stand around the construction site in a hard-hat" (Tu2). Zoning is an important tool not only for housing policy but also for influencing the quality of construction, the use of sustainable technologies, or climate considerations in general (Ta1, Ta6, Ta8, O4, O6): "[Demand for sustainable construction] must come from outside, and in practice, I think it's zoning where it can be required. You get what you ask for, so I think zoning is absolutely essential; nothing extra comes [from the constructors] if it's not required" (Ta1).

3.1 Municipal Policy and Priorities

In the past, climate and housing policies in Finland have been perceived as separate sectors, but one interviewee points out that they are now more linked to each other (O7). Then again, some Finnish interviewees hope for closer cooperation between the different sectors (Tu6, O9): "The left hand could know more precisely what the right hand is doing" (Tu6). Climate and housing policies in Germany are perceived as a patchwork quilt, "and you can't see which grid is being used" (Mz4). On the one hand, there is talk of a lack of transparency in the departments, and it is not known what the building authorities do "behind closed doors, which concepts they approve, i.e. which building permits are granted" (Mz4). For example, decisions are not transparent for the building committee (Mz4), although a lot could be done in terms of climate policy within this framework (Mz5). On the other hand, it is noted that this is a "coincidental interplay" (Mz4) between the departments involved, which is why there was a desire for a special office between climate and all other departments (Mz4). Additionally, in Germany, the policy areas of housing and climate are often situated in different departments, usually in combination with other policy areas. This makes it difficult to cooperate or co-ordinate the creation of housing while taking climate policy aspects into account.

In Finland, there are no remarks on the lack of transparency between departments, but interviewees reflect on institutional trust in other ways. They express both distrust and strong trust in civil servants who are largely responsible for executing zoning (Tu5, Tu7, Tu9, Ta5, Ta7, Ta10). Some suggest that the lack of resources in these departments or the amount of increasing bureaucracy challenge sustainable housing or urban planning (Tu7, Tu9, Tu10, Ta7). One Finnish interviewee (Tu9) also expresses concerns about the "fragmentation" of regional and national politics: the larger lines of decision-making change drastically from election to election, making long-term policies difficult to achieve. This also led him to consider the role of civil servants as essential, as they are capable of creating more long-term change. Many Finnish interviewees would like to see housing policies that consider the entire urban environment and the future in terms of tens if not hundreds of years (Ta2, Ta8, Ta9, Tu5, Tu9, O8). There is, however, a wish to see that housing policy can not only be made long-term but that it can also evolve with time and needs (K3).

The German interviews highlight that ecological aspects are not among the main interconnections in housing policy (K5), which is stated by three key points that must be present in a flat: the connection to a good infrastructure (doctors, kindergartens, schools, etc.), the structural condition and the rental costs (K5). On the other hand, there are also voices that express a clear need to think about the two policy areas together: "We can't think about one and the other" (Mz4), and therefore it is difficult to prioritise one of the two policy areas (Mz4); nevertheless, the housing problem is "number one and must be solved ecologically" (Mz4).

Opinions differ on the extent to which the two policy areas are linked at the local policy level: Some say that the combination of climate and housing policy "correctly" plays an "outstanding role" (W1, W5), others share the opinion that it has (still) not done enough (Mz5), and others speak of a patchwork (K2). One explanation for linking the two policy areas is the fact that climate and the environment nowadays do receive significantly more attention in general than in the past (Mz3).

Some councillors refer to the tension in creating a living space from the social and ecological perspectives (K1, K5, Mz2, Mz4, W5), outlining, for example, that on the one hand, more living space must be created, while at the same time asking *how* this can be achieved in times of climate crisis (K1), as no "grey energy" is to be released (K1), and "building is just CO2, just releases greenhouse gas" (K1). According to this, the question is how to achieve a "sensible compromise" (K1). The question of "do we have to create new building land or how can we manage redensification measures" is described as a central conflict on the local level (W1).

The comments from another interviewee indicate that the creation of (affordable) living space is prioritised at a political level "before anyone at the building authority [...] thinks about whether a building or neighbourhood is at the best energy standard" (K5). This depiction describes the seemingly fundamental trade-off between housing and climate (K5 and others) that prevails in Germany, as it appears that some councillors see an antagonism between the creation of sustainable and social housing (W2). In Finland, this type of antagonism does not arise, but many interviewees—even from "greener" parties—understandably prioritise social sustainability of housing. One interviewee comments on the issue: "You also need to be honest about the fact that few politicians want a story in the papers that says, for example, 'this politician thinks there should be no housing for the poor'. In other words, in politics, we think a lot about what is good and necessary, but we also think a lot about what looks good" (Ta1). What is expected of councillors or what they expect of their own political career might affect the issues they cover or prioritise.

Both German and Finnish municipalities have the urban right of first refusal/pre-emption,[1] which enables a municipality to buy land for urban development purposes that was originally intended to be transferred between private parties. This is intended to influence the future construction and further utilisation of the property. However, it was only in Germany that this right came up as a measure or instrument to link the two policy areas. In an interview, this instrument is described as part of a "sustainable land policy" (W3) in that the city can "intervene a little more itself in the process" in this way. This is described as a "long-term goal" (W3).

3.2 The Technical Dimensions of Housing

A large number of Finnish councillors want sustainability values, such as quality and life cycle, to be considered in both housing design and construction phases to minimise emissions and wasting of resources. Many feel the criteria for climate-resilient construction have become stricter, and building plans that do not account for climate change at all could no longer pass (Ta4, Ta10, Tu6, Tu8, Tu10, O1, O2, O3, O4, O6, O7, O9). However, this does not indicate the amount of consideration

---

[1] The technical term is "Vorkaufsrecht der Gemeinde" in German (literally "the right of the municipality to buy ahead"), "etuosto-oikeus" in Finnish and "förköpsrätt" in Swedish.

3.2 The Technical Dimensions of Housing

given to construction. Some interviewees comment that the rate of emissions reduction is too slow compared to the city's aspirations (Ta6, O8), and the issues are not discussed enough in politics (O9, Ta8): "[Sustainable housing] is a wide political issue, which also has dimensions that are not talked about very much—at least not as much as we could or should" (Ta8).

When it comes to a link between housing and climate in Germany, it is primarily technical construction measures that are being debated at a local political level. Regarding construction, one side argues that it is not a question of banning building, but of how to deal with conflicting objectives by weighing the various options (W1). Another person refers to specific local circumstances regarding tension between the creation of living space and the climate, stating that sufficient areas must be left free to ensure ventilation of the city and referring to the situation in the Rhine-Main region (Mz2, Mz8 [five-finger-system]). Another voice focuses less on the explanations of the local conditions and more on the connection between (social) housing and climate while mentioning that it would not be possible "to build social housing or any housing at all without ecological considerations and vice versa" (Mz4), as building housing without taking ecological aspects into account will not achieve anything and will contribute to the city centre no longer being usable (Mz4).

Finnish interviewees prominently bring up a variety of more sustainable building techniques and materials, such as wood construction (Ta1, Ta3, Ta5, Ta7, O4, O5, O6, O10), more ecological concrete (Ta1, Ta2, Ta4, Tu6, O4, O5), or the recycling of building materials (O1, O5, O7, Ta2, Ta4, Ta6, Tu7). However, Finnish councillors recognise that these techniques and materials can be more expensive and take longer time to produce (O4, O6, Ta6, Ta8, Ta9, Ta10): "It's not always possible to choose the most ecological or environmentally friendly option; materials, technologies and ultimately money might stand in the way" (O4). There is also a lack of information on which is even the most sustainable choice in construction (Ta1, Ta2, Ta3, Ta5, Ta6, O10). Sustainability in techniques is also linked to the energy efficiency of new construction (Tu1, Tu2, Ta4, O1, O3, O6, O10).

Land sealing, "a major topic of ongoing debates" (K6), is often viewed critically (W1, W3, W4, Mz1, Mz4) and is associated with local conditions, for example in Wiesbaden. Reference is made above all to the so-called conversion areas, which have been used as headquarters by the American armed forces for decades. Since the war in Ukraine, these areas have become more important from a military point of view, and it is not foreseeable how long this situation will last. The original plan was for the Americans to sell these areas to the federal government, and the city of Wiesbaden could have acquired them at a preferential price so they could be used to create space for housing. The city could have had an influence on the type of housing that could have been built there (luxury housing vs. affordable housing, W1). The use of these areas would not result in any additional sealing in the urban area of Wiesbaden and would fulfil statements like "we don't want any sealing at all" (W1) or "the less, the better for all" (W4). According to one of the interviewees, these areas were designated as "valuable areas" in a previous land use plan, with which "an incredible amount could be done" (W1). Furthermore, the general opinion is that sealing surfaces should be largely avoided in the future (Mz1, Mz4). It has been considered ideal to find enough areas that do not have to be newly sealed but that are already sealed and can be converted or additionally used for the construction of flats (W4).

Along with construction, energy and heating are strongly perceived as a climate issue, and even as the most important tool for climate work by some Finnish interviewees. In the past, heating and energy production have been the main sources of emissions in Finnish cities, but transport has overtaken them in recent years (Tu2) as cities have largely shifted to more renewable energy solutions. It is relevant to know where the heat and energy needed in housing and construction comes from. In both Finland and Germany, these are connected to the size of apartments, i.e. how many square metres and for how many residents the units need to be heated (O1, O5, Ta8).

When energy is discussed in relation to housing, the perspective usually focuses on heating systems. A good example is the 2023 debate about Germany's new heating law, which is intended to pave the way for a switch to climate-friendly heating systems and to move away from fossil fuels. Heat pumps and district heating are being promoted as alternatives to fossil fuels (W1, W4). Finnish cities also offer incentives for more sustainable heating and energy systems, such as solar panels or heat pumps, and the interviewees bring these up frequently. The use of shared energy sources is also mentioned by some of the interviewees and was described as "super important" (Mz5). Reference is also made to best-practice examples in Denmark, specifically Copenhagen, regarding district heating (*Fernwärme*). However, "of course a lot would have to happen" in this regard, and "a lot more would have to be invested to make the housing stock and [...] also the new buildings all climate-neutral" (Mz5). The conflict between ecology and social aspects is also reflected in energy-related statements. One person comments that before the building authority or the department for building "thinks about whether a building or neighbourhood is somehow designed to the best possible energy standard [...] they will simply try to somehow procure as much living space as quickly as possible" (K5). It seems that the demand for housing is displacing the climate aspect.

Some interviewees call for a certain degree of self-sufficiency and increased self-production of energy (Tu3, Tu4, O5, O8). However, there are challenges in land policy, as renewable energy sources such as wind power significantly change the landscape, raising the question of the NIMBY phenomenon: "It is a problem connected to land policy. The landowners are willing because they receive good compensation, but then there are neighbours and others who won't allow it" (Tu3). Fossil fuels are perceived as outdated sources, and it is considered necessary to invest in renewables. Despite their price tag, they will pay for themselves in the long run (Tu2, Tu8, O8). However, the geographical context matters, as the Finnish climate increases the need for intense heating and, on the other hand, certain forms of energy, such as solar energy, are not reliable for a large part of the year (O10, Tu9).

Energy is an issue not only in housing but also in construction, where energy efficiency has recently become an increasingly sought-after priority, primarily motivated by EU and national regulation. Interviewees mention incentives, such as tax deduction (O1, O3, O7, Ta4) and various digital, technological, and automation solutions (Ta4, O9, O10) that can create energy efficiency. One interviewee points out that housing policies and construction can only influence energy efficiency up to a certain point, after which the occupants become responsible for executing that efficiency (Ta4).

In Germany, in addition to addressing the energy aspect in relation to heating, interviewees also referenced energy-efficient construction and the energy-efficient refurbishment of existing buildings (Mz4), and both were widely supported (Mz4, Mz8). However, in constructing new buildings in general, multiple-family dwelling is also interpreted as an "energy-related climate issue" (K1). This interpretation shows an awareness of the climate footprint with regard to materials and energy consumption while constructing. One person points out that 60% of a building's energy is in the building itself when it is built, and 40% is added over the lifetime of the building (Mz8), which evokes the wish "that we just keep the buildings we have and use them for longer, and what could be more sustainable than a house?" (Mz8). As an example of this statement, the person refers to houses in Mainz that have been inhabited for 500 years, which is seen as a good thing and described as "a pretty efficient use of resources" (Mz8).

Additionally, the large stock of old buildings in Germany—which are primarily listed buildings—plays a major role in terms of combining housing and climate, for example in Wiesbaden. The listed buildings pose a major challenge in terms of energy-friendly refurbishment and sustainability in general, as there is less latitude for refurbishment and renewal due to monument protection regulations. It is even much more expensive (W3, W4), and it is also more difficult than with newer buildings, especially with regard to heating requirements (W1). Also, measures such as adding floors on old buildings seem significantly more difficult than with newer buildings.

In Finland, the need for energy efficiency challenges both new and old housing stock; energy use will certainly be more sustainable in new construction, as seen in the cities' newer, more ecological city districts, but old and listed buildings can prove challenging (Tu2, Tu7). The old buildings also create a construction-related problem. In Finland, councillors debate over whether refurbishment or new construction is more climate-friendly, and studies in favour of both can be found (Ta1, Ta2, Ta7, O2, O6, O8). Some feel like too little refurbishment construction is done, and they wish for more incentives to refurbish and for more systematic guidance on what is worth demolishing or refurbishing (Tu2, O5, O9). Overall, there is a desire to more comprehensively consider the climate impacts of demolition and new construction, for example in the form of using circular economy (Tu2, Tu10, O7).

3.3 How to Build, Where to Build?

Councillors in both countries focus not only on the question of how to build, but also *where* to build. As one Finnish interviewee puts it, "where you build determines how ecologically you will be able to live there" (Ta1). The location is connected to redensification, which means densifying the urban fabric with existing buildings or vacant land in already built-up areas used for housing. This densifying can take the form of filling gaps between buildings as well as adding floors to existing ones. Interviewees in all cities mostly see it as a key factor in creating a sustainable city: "A clear choice was made [in the masterplan] that we want redensification because it is the most economically, ecologically, and socially sustainable way to grow as a city" (O1).

According to one interviewee, local political debates in Germany are about whether redensification is pursued in the city centre or on the outskirts (Mz1). It is noted that in Germany, there is no longer much space in the city centre, resulting in redensification that is as environmentally friendly as possible (W3). The contrast between redensification in the heart of the city and expansion to the outskirts also divides Finnish councillors. In Tampere, one interviewee notes that the "easiest" spots for redensification have already been used, which requires flexibility in planning (Ta1).

A German interviewee mentions in this context that "the principle has existed for decades that internal development takes preference over external development" (W1). It has been linked to the aspect of land sealing by stating that "precisely no sealing" is intended (W1). Redensification and new construction close to the city are seen as necessary; otherwise, the municipality would be forced to construct on the outskirts, where open spaces are largely not available, because it "fulfils important climatic functions" (Mz1, Mz5). Constructing or redensification in the outskirts is seen differently than in the city centre (Mz1) and is evaluated as "the wrong way to go" (Mz1). Alternatively, the creation of housing has been advocated for a former shopping centre "as this does not damage nature and does not cause neighbourhood problems, as the shopping centre's surroundings is a car park" (Mz1). This represents a major difference in the implementation of redensification measures in the outskirts (Mz1).

Redensification evokes mixed feelings and arguments among councillors in Finland and Germany. Redensification is generally very popular when it comes to connecting housing and climate (W1, K6, Mz1), which is obvious in the quote, "wherever something can be densified, added, we must do so" (W1), even if this only covers half of the housing needs (W1). One interviewee describes redensification in the sense of adding floors as "highly controversial" (Mz8) and refers to the consequences for social interactions between the (local) residents (Mz8). From an ecological perspective, there would be "many good arguments in favour of this" (Mz8), but social aspects such as opening a window to call the children playing in the sandpit in the inner courtyard for dinner would be made "more difficult" by redensifying upwards (Mz8). According to this point of view, buildings and apartments should be designed with more flexibility and to fit the phases of life (Mz8, W2). This allusion refers to the increase in individual consumption of living space in Germany in recent decades, which is partly due to the fact that older people remain in their flats or houses (which are far too large), even though they no longer need the space (K6, Mz8, W2, W4). There may be various reasons for this, but this

3.3 How to Build, Where to Build?

trend underlines the connection of housing and climate with regard to the fact that large living spaces require a lot of energy (i.e. for heating).

Several Finnish local councillors raise the issue of adaptable and flexible apartments that would better suit the changing life stages of residents. This is related to both existing housing and new design. As in Germany, the issue is linked to having children, children moving out of the nest, and parents ageing: it is hoped that the apartment could be more easily altered to the needs of its residents (O4, O5). This is particularly relevant in more remote areas, such as Oulu, where the population is ageing rapidly and passing away, leaving behind desolated detached houses that do not move in the markets. One interviewee raises the question of how this aesthetical and sustainable issue could be addressed in politics: "You have these old houses, the owners of which have passed away. We should find a good way to deal with the old housing stock, reuse it for future generations or find a programme that would tell you immediately which house is worth demolishing instead of refurbishing" (O9).

One interviewee in Finland finds the research evidence on redensification conflicting, which can be used to justify both increasing and decreasing it (Ta1). On one hand, some Finnish interviewees welcome the discussion about the relationship between redensification and (urban) nature and environment (Tu2, Tu6, Tu7, Ta1, Ta7), while on the other hand, some feel that cities could redensify even more effectively (O5, O8) or are disappointed by the opposition of residents (Ta5). In Germany, another rather critical statement concerning the issue of redensification interpreted as a question of "where to locate/create new housing" refers to the "negative effects on the corresponding cold-air corridors, and of course the warming in the residential complex as such" (W5, Mz2). It is therefore seen as difficult to completely address all concerns (W5). Nevertheless, filling construction gaps or adding residential units to buildings is seen as a way of avoiding sealing.

One interviewee mentions that if one were not prepared to push for redensification in the city centre, the inevitable consequence would be to go out into the suburbs and build there. However, in cities like Mainz, for example, there is not much open space left (Mz1), the urban areas in Mainz and Kiel are "severely limited" (K6, Mz4) and it is questionable whether the open spaces that do exist are suitable for development due to swampy ground in Kiel (K6).

In the interviews, redensification clashes with suburbs being built on the outskirts of the cities. Many Finnish councillors feel that suburbs built "in the middle of forests", where distances are long and mobility relies on private motoring, are outdated, and would not perhaps be built on the same scale anymore (Ta1, Ta2, Ta5, Ta9, Ta10, Tu6, O8). But the rapid growth of Tampere, for example, requires expansion of the city and building of new suburbs, so they demand the most sustainable design in terms of mobility and plot sizes (Ta2, Ta5). The direction and pace of the city's expansion is a climate-related issue, as rapidly growing and developed areas are at risk of becoming deserted if they cannot attract new populations in the future (O8). Building higher does come up in every Finnish city, but it is mentioned especially in Oulu as a trend in recent years (O2, O3). It is something that strongly divides councillors and parties for and against (Tu4, Tu7, Tu9, O1).

While redensification in the way of topping up is "not possible everywhere and at all times" (K6), even when it is not able "to solve the problem completely" (K6) and it also has an influence on the climatic situation in a city district (W4), it is evaluated positively in alleviating the problem (W4, K6, Mz1). It is seen as an opportunity to create additional living space (Mz1). It has also been expressed that one way of implementing sustainable housing policy is to plan and build according to geographical and local circumstances (W1) or that construction should be adapted to local peculiarities (Mz2). One argument in favour of this was that construction should not take place in areas that would be submerged during heavy rainfall events and that there should be some retention areas (W1).

The question of whether to build multi-floor buildings or to continue building detached/terraced houses is seen as an "ideological issue" (Mz2). Social democrats in Germany have stated that "the days of designating land for detached houses are simply over" (Mz2), and a condition for new construction could be seen in constructing multi-family dwellings wherever possible, including at the edge of the city centre, as this would create more living space in a smaller area and is ultimately a climate issue (K1). Regarding the construction of detached or semi-detached houses with gardens, others point out that these should only be financially affordable if people "move 80 kilometres away" (Mz5). There are comments in favour of single-family-houses too. These are justified, among other things, by the fact that these "small-scale structures" are needed and that no "sardine cans" are wanted, and there is also a desire for fresh air (Mz8). In this context, it is also mentioned that the opposition could allow itself to say such things. Some Finnish interviewees also report a change in housing ideals, which may mean that families are not that keen on living in detached houses or that different housing options are being introduced (Ta2, Ta8). Councillors express a strong need for family housing in Finnish cities, as small apartments in recent years have been overpowering construction. All cities struggle with citizens wanting more family-suitable apartments and detached houses in less dense areas. In the context of the need for family housing, there is little discussion around the climate impact of larger apartments.

In Finnish interviews, there is mostly a strong consensus on seeing the urban fabric designed to be compact and within the existing infrastructure. Transport is the largest source of emissions in all the studied Finnish cities, and ambitious targets and strategies have failed to reduce it at a sufficient pace (Ta1, Ta8, Ta9, Tu2, O3, O5). Transport is perceived as part of the intersection between housing and climate, as it determines how people move in their daily lives. Therefore, it is important to develop efficient public transport (Tu1, Tu2, Ta2, Ta4, O3, O4) along public transport links (Ta1, Ta9, Ta10, Tu6, O5) and have urban development designed for sustainable transport (O4, O5)—or to better enable living in the city without a car (Tu3, O1, O5).

The majority of Finnish councillors want sustainable transport (public transport, walking, and cycling) to be developed. For decades, Oulu has done proactive work with sustainable transport in the form of cycling, for example by improving winter cycling facilities and creating cycle lanes (O2, O4, O6, O7). There are also mentions of the electrification of public transport or private cars, for example by enabling

3.4 Housing Versus Urban Nature

electric charging in apartment buildings and urban planning (Tu2, Tu6, O1, O6, O7, O9, Ta9). Many of the German interviewees link the policy fields of housing and climate with the policy field of transport too (Mz3, W1, K4, W2, W4, W5). The main things mentioned are good transport infrastructure, transport concepts, and the need to link planning and transport policy. One person claims that housing also involves traffic (W2), while another states that housing construction goes hand in hand with traffic infrastructure (W4). Additionally, it is mentioned that transport policy is indirectly also housing policy (Mz3).

With regard to the creation of new living space in the form of new buildings, the so-called parking space statutes in Germany, which regulate the number of parking spaces for cars and bicycles on the respective property or in the vicinity, play an important role. These statutes are said to be considered (W3) especially in the context of redensification measures such as the addition of floors or a gap development. If the required space for cars and bicycles cannot be provided within the construction project, these regulations can be a barrier for the measures. At the same time, this statute symbolises the fact that in Germany, the law still focuses on private and individual transport. Some Finnish respondents also feel that urban transport policy is "sabotaged" by focusing too much on private cars (O5, O8, Ta9): "We are in a difficult situation because we have made ambitious [climate] goals, but in politics these goals are constantly being sabotaged by private motoring solutions" (Ta9). Oulu has made efforts to reduce the priority of private cars and parking space in the city structure (O1).

3.4 Housing Versus Urban Nature

Finnish councillors often bring up green areas and the environment in the context of housing, although it is more linked to wellbeing, urban aesthetics, and even biodiversity protection than to climate change mitigation or adaptation. Parks, green areas, local or urban nature, and green urban fabric in general are considered important by citizens and councillors alike. German local councillors occasionally mention green areas such as parks and green spaces, and they consider them to be important. Rather, open spaces, as areas not yet built upon, are claimed to fulfil an important climatic function (Mz1).

There is a dilemma that redensification is beneficial for climate change but that it simultaneously reduces the amount of nature and green areas in the city. Many Finnish councillors also suggest that this displeases many inhabitants too (Ta1, Ta3, Ta7, Tu2, Tu6, Tu7, O8, O9, O10). Zoning and urban design should strive to ensure that densification does not just generate a city made of pure concrete (Tu6, Ta6): "It's nice that the committee also ensures that there are sufficient green areas and vegetation so that the urban environment has (a) shade and (b) moisture, both of which help to keep the built environment much more pleasant on hot summer days" (Ta6). In Mainz, one interviewee also confirms this: "In my opinion, Mainz should actually be a really green city, you should see more green than grey. Of course, at the moment, it's exactly the other way around" (Mz4).

Constructing in more remote areas and the resulting loss of nature (Tu6, O7, O8) is also identified as a problem by Finnish interviewees. Redensification is seen as an alternative, more environmental option as it "sacrifices little of the urban nature in order to preserve 'real' nature further away" (Tu6). However, Finnish councillors hope to find the delicate balance between redensification and green areas.

However, only some interviews recognise the importance of green areas in climate change adaptation or mitigation, as they are rather related to the quality of housing and living. Adaptation comes up with the mention that greener cities retain stormwater, provide shade, and protect against the urban heat island effect (Ta1, Tu6, Ta6, Ta8). A German interviewee says that "every litre of water that goes into greening the city also benefits the cooling of the city [...] and the money is not poured away" (Mz4).

Finnish councillors have mixed views on green roofs and similar façade greening measures; some consider them to be beneficial and see them bringing welcomed aestheticism into the city (Ta6, Tu6, Tu7, O6, O9), while others question their cost–benefit ratio or have concerns about who will maintain them (Tu9, Tu10). In Germany, there is criticism that measures such as greening should finally be taken seriously (K6), and there are some mentions that urban greening hasn't been realised due to the cost argument (K6, Mz4).

Some refer to measures such as green roofs and façades or environmentally friendly materials (K6, Mz2) as part of the link between climate and housing or as climate protection measures (K4) for the urban climate, citing best-practice examples such as Barcelona (K6) or Aarhus (K5). Interviewees in Turku are also impressed by the sustainability and greening measures of Copenhagen that had been witnessed on a field trip (Tu4, Tu5, Tu7). One German interviewee refers to the high costs (Mz2), which can be interpreted as a barrier to integrating climate and housing policy, while another interviewee describes greening measures in the contexts of climate and housing or sustainable housing as German "standard issues" (Mz5). These measures seem to enjoy a lot of positive support due to the cooling effect and the comparatively "simple" implementation (Mz5, K6, Mz4), and they should be taken more seriously (K6).

3.5 Missing Ambitions

Interviewees rarely mention the future unless asked directly. This is reflected in how little they raise the issues of climate change adaptation, the circular economy, or future development in general. It also indicates that rapid political action with visible decisions is a priority.

When councillors discuss climate change, it is mainly linked to mitigation with only few visions of what changes and adaptation measures cities will have to take. Some recognise the general challenges of climate change: Finnish councillors

3.5 Missing Ambitions

mostly mention floods, which challenge stormwater management and also impacts the areas where and *how* building can occur (Ta1), whereas German councillors mostly mention local peculiarities, such as the risk of heavy rainfall events for certain parts of the city (W1), drought and forest fires.

The increasing heat waves and the urban heat island effect is an increasing threat in the future that will affect the type of housing we build (Ta1, Ta6, Ta8; Mz8, K1). Techniques and construction in the future must consider air conditioning and sufficient cooling of apartments, which is a big change in Finland, where protection from cold has always been a more significant housing issue: "Now we are starting to get to a place where we may not want the natural heat [and light] so much. So far, the cold has been a bigger problem than heat, but the heat may be more challenging in the future" (Ta1).

German interviewees reference the role of cold-air corridors not only in new construction or redensification projects but also in general with regard to the, for example, the boxed-in location of Mainz and Wiesbaden (Mz1, Mz8, W1). These fresh-air corridors are intended to bring fresh air into the hot city centre, which was not always considered (Mz8). This shows that some councillors are sensitised to upcoming climate changes and are integrating them into their statements.

The topic of space is also mentioned in connection with climatic aspects. The function of open spaces for the urban climate is mentioned and described as "important" (Mz1, Mz2), probably referring to the cooling effect of open spaces on the urban climate. As a broader urban development solution to both flooding and heat, Finnish councillors propose more sufficient green spaces to provide humidity, shade, and water absorption (Ta1, Ta6, Ta8). One interviewee in Wiesbaden considers it important to make rooftop greening obligatory to "become not only a sustainable city but also a water-storing one" (W2). So greening measures are seen as an important adaptation measure in both countries, although they are mentioned quite rarely. One Finnish interviewee also briefly mentions specific weather phenomena, such as diagonal rain, as factors affecting housing design and construction (Ta1).

Waste management, recycling, and material efficiency are perceived as a part of housing and climate policy, but they are surprisingly underrepresented in the data compared to their importance and prevalence in the policy documents. Circular economy and land recycling play a minor role in the interviews, although many interviewees feel that the circular economy has a huge potential that has not yet been realised in practice (Ta2, Ta6, Ta9, Tu7, Tu10, O5, O7). Circular economy can be seen as an economic system that creates efficiency through recycling and reuse instead of producing new (Sitra, 2022, 38–39).

In Germany, circular economy is interpreted by only two persons from Wiesbaden as an ideal to strive for in the future (W1, W4). The municipality should develop a land policy "that should lead to land recycling in the long term" (W1). Ideally, this should be organised in such a way that something is only (re)sealed where something is unsealed at the same time (W1, W4). In this context, a shift away from the demolition of buildings is also expressed by the mantra that "practically nothing" should be demolished (W4). Tampere emerges in the interviews as the only city where councillors knew of circular economy criteria having been used in a plot competition (Ta1, Ta4). One interviewee in Turku mentions the Kakola heat pump plant, which produces renewable energy through waste heat from wastewater (Tu2), and one interviewee in Oulu briefly references the material recycling centre of Välimaa, which deals with recycling construction waste (O7).

Given that both climate change adaptation and implementation of circular economy require broader and long-term visioning, it comes as no surprise how little councillors talk about the broader systemic cultural change that is needed—the just transition towards a post-carbon society. In Finland, interestingly, this contrasts with the 2022 energy crisis, which was still somewhat topical at the time of the interviews despite having been shorter and milder than first expected. The Europe-wide energy crisis was mainly the result of the war in Ukraine. Many countries in Europe received gas, coal, and oil from Russia, but because of the sanctions, it was decided to stop the import of energy supplies from Russia. This led to a rapid rise in energy prices, calls to save energy, and national governments and the EU taking action through regulations and emergency plans. However, the energy crisis also seemed to underline how society and individuals are just waiting for the crisis to be over to get "back to normal". Many interviewees link this to the spike in prices and the economic situation—once that eased up, the crisis could be forgotten (for example, Ta8).

The few interviewees with some visions of the future explicitly mention the lack of it in local politics. There are reports of an inability to imagine or execute different aesthetic, architectural, transportation, or urban planning solutions (Tu2, O5, Ta8). One interviewee questions the kind of city and housing that policymakers want to create and enable: "The vision of what kind of city, how people will move around in their daily lives in 30 years' time, is a hazy picture, and perhaps it is best described by thinking that the way people do things now will go on forever" (Ta8). This is also reflected in the German interviews: "Those who are responsible do not have a really vivid picture of what will happen in 30 years" (Mz4). Planning and visioning for the future is linked to climate change adaptation: how can construction be planned so that it does not take decades for the city and environment to recover?

One interviewee mentions how merely following and reacting to trends takes apart the possibility to imagine something new—how things should or even could be constructed (Ta8). Interesting new architectural proposals are emerging, such as modern, more ecological, and wooden-built townhouse housing, but the rigid policy mechanisms and the political reluctance to guide housing prevents these possibilities from flourishing (Tu2, O5). One interviewee in Turku (Tu7) mentions the importance of citizens being aware of and influencing the city development, which can happen, for example, through open consultations. However, they also recognise that it is difficult to bring information to the attention of citizens and to get them to seize the opportunity to have an impact.

From the perspective of a German interviewee, it becomes "tricky" in general when it comes to changing existing structures, as this involves asking people "to change one or two behaviours", as this is always "difficult" in politics (Mz3). The inability to respond to the need for change is also linked to climate denialism, which some Finnish interviewees identify in local politics. This can manifest as outright disbelief, but also as an unwillingness to invest in green solutions (Tu6) or as questioning how much Finland's climate actions matter on a global scale (O10). Some do suggest that residents are already demanding the most sustainable building and housing possible (Tu6) or that green transition is also a market advantage (Ta1, Ta9). Only one interviewee mentions the importance of taking care of workers in less sustainable sectors (Ta7) or considering the idea that the green transition should also be socially sustainable and just.

Reference

Sitra. (2022). *Tackling root causes – Halting biodiversity loss through the circular economy*. Sitra studies 205. Retrieved December 18, 2024, from https://media.sitra.fi/app/uploads/2022/05/sitra-tackling-root-causes-2.pdf

Open Access This chapter is licensed under the terms of the Creative Commons Attribution 4.0 International License (http://creativecommons.org/licenses/by/4.0/), which permits use, sharing, adaptation, distribution and reproduction in any medium or format, as long as you give appropriate credit to the original author(s) and the source, provide a link to the Creative Commons license and indicate if changes were made.

The images or other third party material in this chapter are included in the chapter's Creative Commons license, unless indicated otherwise in a credit line to the material. If material is not included in the chapter's Creative Commons license and your intended use is not permitted by statutory regulation or exceeds the permitted use, you will need to obtain permission directly from the copyright holder.

Chapter 4
Wicked Problems at the Crossroads: Integrating Housing and Climate Policy for Sustainable Futures

4.1 Integration of Housing and Climate Policy as a Wicked Problem

The analysis shows how climate and housing policy sectors integrate in a municipal context, but it also reveals dead spots where integration is not yet sufficiently realised. Cooperation between policy sectors is always needed for successful policy integration (Tosun & Lang, 2017). Research on policy integration has shown beneficial results, as it might help accomplish intersecting objectives or allow policymakers to approach overall objectives instead of focusing on individual sectoral objectives (Stead & de Jong, 2006, 4). Newell (2004, 121) has argued that policy integration would be not only the most economical but also the most effective way to pursue climate protection.

As the combined analysis of policy documents from the cities and our interviews with local councillors show, integrated approaches to both housing and climate challenges can be considered a wicked problem not only from the scientific perspective but also from the viewpoint of councillors. The combination of housing and climate policy as a wicked problem emerges from a complex interplay of various interconnected and conflicting issues.

Municipal policies often reflect an inconsistency in climate and housing targets due to ideological divides and political compromises. The nature of local politics requires compromise and tolerance of party differences, often creating solutions that do not entirely satisfy anyone. However, Arman et al. (2009, 3040) claim that the tension surrounding discussions on sustainability indicates the issue is advancing and keeps the discussion running. Smaller parties in particular must be very conscious of which "battles they choose": to advance one issue on their agenda, they might have to bend on many others. The personal power of single councillors is usually limited. The councillors' challenge of balancing ecological goals with economic and social demands leads to tensions.

Sustainable construction techniques, such as wood or recycled materials, are identified as solutions yet face obstacles like higher costs and limited production capacity. The topic creates tension between Finnish councillors over whether the city should control sustainable construction regulations more or less. Many identify that more comprehensive guidance could lead to stricter sustainability criteria, which in turn could help the integration of the two sectors. Both in Finland and Germany, energy efficiency measures and novel energy solutions are crucial but usually come at a financial premium, creating a trade-off between economic feasibility and ecological responsibility and showcasing the systemic difficulty in balancing innovative construction with feasibility.

Decisions on where to build—whether through redensification in urban centres or expansion into greenfield sites—pose ecological and social dilemmas. Redensification is considered in both countries as a key instrument in the development of more sustainable cities and housing and is justified on the grounds of climate, economic, and social sustainability. This does not come as a surprise since academia broadly discusses redensification and its connection to sustainability (e.g. Wicki & Kaufmann, 2022; Angelo & Wachsmuth, 2020; Artmann et al., 2019). But even though redensification supports sustainability by preserving natural landscapes from new construction, it potentially reduces the availability of green spaces that contribute to climate adaptation as well as to the wellbeing of the residents. Conversely, expanding into remote areas may undermine climate targets by increasing car dependency and contributing to land sealing, yet adding natural areas for cooling and flood mitigation. This duality exemplifies the wicked problem, as each option carries both benefits and substantial drawbacks. Where to build raises practical but also ideological and normative questions: how high to build, where in the city, and how to connect transport to housing?

In techniques, construction and redensification, integration of housing and climate is challenged by knowledge-related factors, such as the most sustainable techniques or aforementioned redensification. The question accounts for councillors' resources and the quantity, quality, and comprehensibility of the information that they receive. As laymen, councillors are, by definition, not professionals, and they depend on the information municipal administration provides.

Finally, short-term political actions often take precedence over more sustainable, future-oriented policies. Even if some interviewees mention climate change adaptation or circular economy, there still seems to be insufficient commitment to long-term sustainability decisions and more focus on rapid political action or decisions with visible "results". Considering the emissions and natural resources that construction requires (e.g. European Union, 2024), a more coherent organisation of the circular economy within construction and land use will become necessary in the future. Although Finnish interviewees praise the future potential of the circular economy, it is not seen as adequately embedded in policy, and interviewees have no vision on how to improve its implementation.

Short-sightedness in future-oriented policies can prevent the development of integrated strategies that could effectively address both climate and housing needs over decades. The findings highlight that discussions around future adaptation

4.1 Integration of Housing and Climate Policy as a Wicked Problem   53

measures and the broader systemic shifts required for a post-carbon society are limited, further entrenching the complexity of the problem.

The councillors are aware of the desired connection between housing and climate policy sectors. However, this does not seem to affect the internal administrative setup of the municipalities that is necessary for a deeper, more legitimate integration and cooperation between the two fields. The interviews reveal a general lack of agreement not only on how to build, but *how much* and *where* to build in the most sustainable and climate-friendly way. The extent to which the sectors are integrated, and the importance of achieving this, is something on which councillors have different views.

In the following, we further discuss the characteristics of integrating housing and climate and how it materialised through the wicked problems framework (see Sect. 2.1).

First, as expected, councillors struggle to formulate the problems at stake convincingly, and there is no overarching agreement between the persons involved regarding where the problem (integration of housing and climate policy) begins and where it ends. Since both housing and climate are wicked problems in themselves, with multiple overlaps into third policy realms and countless interactions, it is no wonder that the integration of both fields seems like an overwhelming problem to address and solve. The question also addresses how much consideration is given to climate change in municipal policy, as according to wicked problems, different groups can have multiple opinions as well as conflicting interests on the issue. Party attitudes and ideologies influence this case regarding costs or responsibilities that lie with countries. Stead and de Jong (2006) argue how important political cohesion and leader-level commitment are for integration. Both climate change and housing policy emerge in the interview data as issues where councillors' objectives may be in line, but the means conflict.

Second, wicked problems, by definition, are ever-changing. This is especially true for housing and climate, where new technologies, policies, economic conditions, and environmental realities constantly shift the policy landscape. Due to evolving context issues, both housing and climate policy are "moving targets", which is even more true for the integration of the two areas. Politicians are unclear about where the problem starts, where a possible "final" solution can be and how it can be achieved. This is especially true for the German cases, where politicians from the housing field feel that cities are overwhelmed with population growth in the sense that they "build, build, build", but housing never seems to be enough in the eyes of the public, especially renters.

The complex nature and lack of clear solutions for wicked problems challenge integration. Since the concrete is usually considered more acute than the abstract, councillors may find it easier to make policy decisions related to housing rather than climate. With housing, it is easier to measure action and monitor progress than with more abstract climate goals. Alongside that, climate change is only one aspect in policymaking: as a major (and in many cases acute) political issue, housing involves a wide range of different and divergent interests and needs (Ohisalo, 2018, 331). Often, the aspect of social and economic sustainability becomes a priority. This is also clear in the interviews in the way the social aspect dominates housing policy in both countries and how social and ecological sustainability are contrasted, especially in the German context.

Additionally, since housing and climate are considered policy fields with inertia, consequences of decisions (as well as non-decisions) cannot be easily assessed and addressed. For example, newly built housing units may combat the housing shortage in the short term, but negatively impact climate in the long run. Vice versa, short-term climate adaptation measures, e.g. preservation of cold-air corridors, may have the intended effect, but at the same time, they can form a barrier to developing much-needed housing in the area in question. Finally, there is no chance to run a test if an implemented measure was "right or wrong" because even successful integration of housing and climate policy might well be by chance or because there are extraordinary circumstances that cannot be adapted to other circumstances.

The problem of integrating housing and climate policy can be considered as quite unique on two levels: the problem has not been addressed before, or there is no standard "one-size-fits-all" solution. It is also obvious that there is no room for manoeuvre in both policy areas. It is clear for local actors that they can neither sit out the lack of housing nor the effects of climate change, but the required integrated decision is complex, and a wrong decision in one of the two areas could result in non-accomplishment in both.

Further, as councillors frequently pointed out, the inability to solve the housing and climate issue in an integrated way can be a symptom of a multitude of other problems. Barriers to integrated solutions, for example, are partly a consequence of the setup of the local administration. Most of them are organised using the department logic and not completed by a problem-centred perspective where needed. This means that housing and climate policy are almost always the responsibility of different units within the local administration. This is especially true for the German cases: As councils tend to build up their committees to match the administrative structure, it is difficult to overcome silo mentality in general—if there are already silos in the setup of the municipal administration, they might also cause silos in the political sphere. In both countries, some interviewees recognise a lack of cross-sectoral cooperation between policy areas, which could be connected to the silo effect phenomenon (Scott & Gong, 2021). The lack of housing and climate adaption/mitigation measures can also be seen as a symptom of the economy focused on growth or as a final consequence of population growth, the growth of living standards (i.e. usage of housing space per capita), or just as a lack of prioritising these policy areas.

To summarise, each aspect brought up by the interviewees—from policy inconsistencies and technical challenges to urban planning conflicts and limited future visioning—underscores how combining housing and climate policies intertwines economic, social, and ecological dimensions. The inherent trade-offs and competing interests at play reinforce the characterisation of this policy combination as a wicked problem, defined by its resistance to simple solutions and the need for multifaceted approaches including collaborative and adaptive governance and integrating diverse fields like urban planning, architecture, engineering, economics, and social sciences (e.g. Campbell, 2016).

Termeer et al. (2019, 176) remark that the wicked problems theory has been criticised for being difficult to utilise in policy, although originally it was not only intended for an academic context. A problem portrayed as wicked challenges policymakers: they have to question how to deal with or let alone solve an issue that has been characterised as virtually impossible to resolve (see Noordegraaf et al., 2019). Successful integration of the two policy sectors requires changing existing social behaviours, economic structures, and regulatory frameworks. This can face resistance from those who benefit from the status quo, such as developers who prioritise profits over sustainability or homeowners who fear property value loss due to regulatory changes (e.g. Geels, 2014; Frank, 2020; Martiskainen et al., 2021). The concept of wicked problems could be used in a more analytical way, mending critique of the theory and complementary theories to further develop the concept (Termeer et al., 2019, 177). This could clarify not only the theory but the different ways in which wicked problems can be tackled in practice.

4.2 Reflections for the Future

The need for an ambitious and widespread cultural shift towards sustainability is linked to visioning the future, adapting to climate change and organising our economy differently. Green economy is an alternative that creates social sustainability while also considering the environment, climate change, and sufficiency of natural resources (UNEP, 2024). The concept is closely connected with other economic alternatives such as circular economy or bio economy, even though they do not share similar strategies (D'Amato et al., 2017).

A green economy requires strong leadership, a shared vision, and both short- and long-term measures in policymaking. In addition, with the changes, the system must be resilient and capable of adapting to challenges (Antikainen et al., 2013). The challenge is how to make long-term, effective climate policy when the future affected by climate change is intangible and uncertain and requires an enormous amount of trust in the measures taken.

A just ecological transition could also find sustainable ideas from the circular economy (see Riekkinen et al., 2020). The fact that councillors only rarely mentioned circular economy is not surprising, since although Finnish municipalities have strived to meet the growing objectives of the circular economy through different programmes and plans, they are not automatically incorporated into construction or land use policy. This requires adequate resources, a willingness to change current practices, expert knowledge, and political guidance (Vierikko et al., 2020).

Circular economy in land use planning is connected to different sections: green areas and biodiversity conservation, reuse of materials, energy efficiency and renewable energy production, and effective waste management (Vierikko et al., 2020). The recycling of construction materials is an obvious link between the circular economy and housing, which was discussed to a certain extent by some Finnish interviewees, for example in the form of material recycling centres. Recycling, reinventing different ways of usage and a communal, sharing-based circular economy could be considered in housing policy.

Cities in general pursue growth, and the interviews mostly do not challenge the growth paradigm, but rather reinforce it in housing. Even with the ideal of sustainable development, our overconsuming and fossil fuel-dependent world has not sufficiently changed. Degrowth offers an alternative with a vision of producing and consuming less and, through that, increasing both social and ecological wellbeing (Martínez-Alier et al., 2010, 1741). It serves as a collective term for a wealth of approaches, concepts, and debates that deal with alternative economic forms and their impact on society and environment (ARL, 2021, 1). Degrowth also extends to the housing sector. Housing is a basic human right, and in the German scientific debate, the focus is on collective forms of housing, sustainability-orientated, and architectural innovations such as housing in cooperatives, rooftop greening, modular construction, and smaller individual living space consumption (ibid., 4). The fact that the issues of climate and housing are closely linked within this debate underlines that degrowth could serve as an inspiration for linking the two policy areas at a local political level in future times. Even if degrowth can be interpreted as a drastic or radical theory, it should at least be considered as a possible approach to housing and climate and their integration.

In terms of ecological sustainability, it is impossible to separate social sustainability from the green future (e.g. Bennett et al., 2019). However, social justice, for example in the case of a workwise just transition, has been identified as a potential brake on the transition (Huttunen & Rekola, 2021, 155). This contradiction between the growth paradigm, sustainable transition, and cultural change is connected to social and ecological sustainability being pitted against each other; and in the case of housing, the social comes first. Although an understandable priority, just transition cannot be a weapon or constraint on environmental and climate policy objectives. In that case, it will always be forced to bend in the face of economic and social sustainability, and genuine, long-term change or sustainability cannot be achieved (ibid., 161).

While some councillors speak of national and international regulation, there is less talk about forces outside politics, such as individual citizens, civil society, or companies. Policymakers have limited means to execute sustainable housing or analyse how companies adopt climate work in their action. Information flow and close cooperation, which should also be visible to every citizen, is important. The Finnish cities have climate "programmes" (such as the Climate League in Turku or Climate Partners in Tampere) that aim to involve citizens and businesses in climate action. Several networks, such as the Climate Leadership Coalition (CLC) in Finland, also offer cooperation and networking between different actors such as businesses, universities, or municipalities, and Turku and Tampere are participants.

Finnish interviewees mentioned that the energy crisis had shaken up structures and required rapid action to adapt. Countries that had proactively invested in renewable energy sources coped better with the shock compared to countries that were more dependent on fossil fuels. In the wake of the energy crisis, the European Union has committed to increasing renewable energy, which suggests recognition of its essential role in preparing for future crises (Holman & Siemplenski Lefort, 2024). The crisis has made new renewable technologies visible in policymaking, and interviewees expressed a desire to explore them more. Due to the energy crisis and mild weather, household energy consumption in 2022 was lower than in previous years (StatFin, 2023). Many Finnish interviewees also noted that it was relatively easy for citizens to reduce their energy consumption. The critical nature and abruptness of the energy crisis called for rapid action, pushing both the discussion and concrete projects of renewable energy forward. How is it possible to bring the same sense of urgency into climate-related policymaking when the challenges are not directly related to the price tag of next winter but to the winters of the next decades and centuries? Ignoring the political, economic, ecological, and social changes caused by climate change is easier when the effects are not yet too disruptive in central or northern Europe.

Although the studied cities recognise the risks posed by climate change, they have only become explicitly visible in Finland in recent years, so there has been less pressure to consider climate adaptation. Keeping this and Finland's lack of systematically monitored climate change adaptation in mind, the topic not surfacing often in the interviews does not come as a surprise. The pressure to consider adaptation and to monitor the measures has recently increased through the national Finnish Climate Act and international agreements (Hildén et al., 2022, 108). The challenge, however, does not only lie within the fact that the effects of climate change have not been that noticeable in Finland so far, but also that research on construction and adaptation has focused more on overheating than, for example, on responding to increased rainfall, and the research on colder regions and their adaptation measures is lacking (Stagrum et al., 2020). While cities increasingly work on tackling climate change, there is the need to better integrate mitigation with adaptation. Previous research suggests several paths towards better integration, for example by fully concentrating mitigation and adaptation techniques in one single administrative unit (Kern et al., 2021).

Bierwirth (2021, 172) notes that housing policy demands changes in ecological and social perspectives, and we must think of alternative ways of arranging our housing. The issue of social sustainability was raised by many interviewees, for example in the wish that people of different income levels could reside in the same areas or the wish for more communal housing. In Germany especially, the relations between sustainable and social housing were tense, which has been acknowledged in research as well (see, e.g., Arman et al., 2009). The broader cultural shift required by the integration of housing and climate policies cannot overly subordinate ecological values to social values; in the long-term, ecological values and the environment *are* social justice.

4.3 Concluding Words About Policy Integration

The issue of sustainable housing will not solve itself as climate change marches on. As we have shown, the silo effect, issues with knowledge, the scarcity of resources, and the multidisciplinary nature of the problem make integration of climate and housing policy tricky. In his article, Martín (2022, 9) describes homes as nodes that connect both concrete and symbolic ribbons of security, geography, consumption, social networks, culture, and economy, as well as many other factors. Each housing-related node and ribbon is inextricably linked to climate (policy), making it impossible for climate and housing policies to be separated from each other. This leads Martín to call for a policy reform that would better recognise this link.

Many Finnish interviewees feel that all decision-making and every strategy "always" take climate change into account, but they also question *the extent* to which this is done. So there is recognition of integration between climate and other policy sectors, but some do not yet see it as sufficient. Missing consensus on achieving targets, different ideologies and different levels of institutional trust challenge councillors' work and the integration of the sectors. As for the wicked problem angle, ideological differences, the severity of the issue, and the difficulty of identifying where the wicked problem of housing and climate integration begins and ends can make the problem seem impossible to solve.

The issue of "antagonism" between ecological and social sustainability that emerges in Germany should be further discussed, even if the indications of this conflict in the Finnish context were subtler. Research has found conflict or tension between these sustainability dimensions (e.g. Huttunen & Rekola, 2021; Hirvilammi, 2020), so different ways to pursue and measure holistic sustainability of housing should be sought.

Some interviewees describe climate and housing policy as a "patchwork quilt", which would benefit from cross-sectoral cooperation. Additionally, both national and international policy diffusion and different climate networks can help to spread good ideas and advance integration. Motivated leaders and civil servants, who can influence the development of the city, are also key actors.

The interviewees mostly recognised integration of climate and housing policies in relation to construction, technology, energy, and location of housing. However, we found that there is no complete consensus in municipal politics on where to build, let alone how much and the most sustainable ways. The councillors are continuously challenged by the tension between densifying urban structure and declining nature.

In construction, the question of whether enough climate action has been adopted remains. Climate-friendly construction materials and technologies are frequently mentioned, but councillors ponder calculation methods and how to increase their use in the industry. Financial resources and political guidance can encourage linking housing and climate policy at both policy and practical levels. Stricter legislation, political guidance or financial drivers can urge constructors to choose more sustainable construction. However, political guidance requires updated skills and education. One way of achieving that can be found in the cooperation between universities and cities, as in the Turku Urban Research Programme. It is also constantly becoming more crucial to include climate change adaptation into housing policy.

Interviewees widely see redensification as the most sustainable way to grow as a city and create housing, although it generates mixed feelings among both councillors and citizens. It conflicts with green areas, which councillors consider important, especially from a social sustainability perspective, but it also counters climate change. Finnish councillors in particular see planning and zoning as crucial means in creating sustainable housing, as it is so connected with compact urban structure and transport. The challenges of redensification and its impact should be further studied and discussed. It is possible to adopt some compensatory measures, for example green roofs, but preserving more intact nature and urban nature is important for biodiversity and climate, as well as for aesthetics and wellbeing. We also need more research and more coherent policies on the challenging question of whether the most climate-friendly way is to refurbish old buildings or to build completely new ones.

Many practices and habits that have thus far seemed "normal" are beginning to come across as outdated to some councillors, such as combustion-based energy forms. Councillors see the importance of investing in renewable forms of energy; investing now is a long-term choice that will save resources later. This is linked to the kind of future we are creating with our decisions. Some Finnish councillors discussed the climate change adaptation and circular economy, but very few councillors introduced any visions for the future unless asked directly.

Finnish cities have recently shown a growing interest in integrating climate and housing policies. Since the study was conducted, several housing and climate strategies have been updated and have shown more visible interest in the integration. For example, Oulu's land and housing strategy emphasises both ecological and social sustainability, and the city seeks to grow sustainably (City of Oulu, 2024, 17–18). Nevertheless, this shows that although sustainability is embraced, the growth paradigm is not questioned.

Policy integration delivers practical results and offers the opportunity to achieve them across multiple policy sectors (Stead & de Jong, 2006, 20). Newell (2004, 121) urges us to consider climate change as a broader issue for policy choices and sectors that deal with the economy, energy strategy, or housing, rather than as a single, isolated problem. After all, climate change is not just an issue that affects these sectors but a direct result of the decisions taken in them.

References

Angelo, H., & Wachsmuth, D. (2020). Why does everyone think cities can save the planet? *Urban Studies, 57*(11), 2201–2221. https://doi.org/10.1177/0042098020919081

Antikainen, R., Lähtinen, K., Leppänen, M., & Furman, E. (2013). *Vihreä talous suomalaisessa yhteiskunnassa [The green economy in the Finnish society]*. Ympäristöministeriön raportteja

I. Ympäristöministeriö. Retrieved May 18, 2024, from https://julkaisut.valtioneuvosto.fi/bitstream/handle/10138/41446/YMra1_2013_Vihrea_talous_suomalaisessa_yhteiskunnassa.pdf?sequence=2&isAllowed=y

ARL – Akademie für Raumentwicklung in der Leibniz-Gemeinschaft. (2021). *Postwachstum und Raumentwicklung – Denkanstöße für Wissenschaft und Praxis*. [*Post-growth and spatial development - food for thought for science and practice*]. Positionspapier aus der ARL 122. Retrieved February 15, 2024, from https://www.arl-net.de/system/files/media-shop/pdf/pospapier/pospapier_122.pdf

Arman, M., Zuo, J., Wilson, L., Zillante, G., & Pullen, S. (2009). Challenges of responding to sustainability with implications for affordable housing. *Ecological Economics, 68*(12), 3034–3041. https://doi.org/10.1016/j.ecolecon.2009.07.007

Artmann, M., Inostroza, L., & Fan, P. (2019). Urban sprawl, compact urban development and green cities. How much do we know, how much do we agree? *Ecological Indicators, 96*(2), 3–9. https://doi.org/10.1016/j.ecolind.2018.10.059

Bennett, N. J., Blythe, J., Cisneros-Montemayor, A. M., Singh, G. G., & Sumaila, U. R. (2019). Just transformations to sustainability. *Sustainability, 11*(14), 3881. https://doi.org/10.3390/su11143881

Bierwirth, A. (2021). Wohnraumpolitik versus Umweltpolitik: ein Widerspruch? [Housing policy versus environmental policy: A contradiction?]. In G. Spars (Ed.), *Wohnungsfrage 3.0. Perspektiven auf Gesellschaft und Politik*. W. Kohlhammer GmbH.

Campbell, S. D. (2016). The Planner's Triangle revisited: Sustainability and the evolution of a planning ideal that can't stand still. *Journal of the American Planning Association, 82*(4), 388–397. https://doi.org/10.1080/01944363.2016.1214080

City of Oulu. (2024). *Oulun maankäytön toteuttamisohjelma 2024–2028* [*The Land Use Execution Program of City of Oulu 2024–2028*]. Retrieved December 12, 2024, from https://www.ouka.fi/sites/default/files/attachments/Oulun_Maank%C3%A4yt%C3%B6n_toteuttamisohjelma_2024_2028_sa.pdf

D'Amato, D., Droste, N., Allen, B., Kettunen, M., Lähtinen, K., Korhonen, J., Leskinen, P., Matthies, B. D., & Toppinen, A. (2017). Green, circular, bio economy: A comparative analysis of sustainability avenues. *Journal of Cleaner Production, 168*, 716–734. https://doi.org/10.1016/j.jclepro.2017.09.053

European Union. (2024). *Buildings and construction*. Internal Market, Industry, Entrepreneurship and SMEs. Retrieved December 11, 2024, from https://single-market-economy.ec.europa.eu/industry/sustainability/buildings-and-construction_en

Frank, K. (2020). Accepting climate denial and loss: Florida's lessons for pragmatic adaptation. In M. Scott, & M. Lennon (Eds.), Climate disruption and planning: Resistance or retreat? *Planning Theory & Practice, 21*(1), 125–154.

Geels, F. W. (2014). Regime resistance against low-carbon transitions: Introducing politics and power into the multi-level perspective. *Theory, Culture & Society, 31*(5), 21–40. https://doi.org/10.1177/0263276414531627

Hildén, M., Tikkakoski, P., Sorvali, J., Mettiäinen, I., Käyhkö, J., Helminen, M., Määttä, H., Berninger, K., Meriläinen, P., Ahonen, S., Kolstela, J., Juhola, S., Tynkkynen, O., Gregow, H., Groundstroem, F., Halonen, J. I., Munck af Rosenschöld, J., Tuomenvirta, H., Carter, T., Lehtonen, H., Luomaranta, A., & Mäkelä, A. (2022). *Ilmastonmuutokseen sopeutuminen Suomessa – nykytila ja kehitysnäkymät* [*Adaptation to climate change in Finland – The current state and development outlooks*]. Valtioneuvoston selvitys- ja tutkimustoiminnan julkaisusarja 2022:55. Valtioneuvosto. Retrieved December 8, 2023, from https://julkaisut.valtioneuvosto.fi/bitstream/handle/10024/164300/VNTEAS_2022_55.pdf?sequence=1&isAllowed=y

Hirvilammi, T. (2020). The virtuous circle of sustainable welfare as a transformative policy idea. *Sustainability (Basel, Switzerland), 12*(1). https://doi.org/10.3390/su12010391

References

Holman, R., & Siemplenski Lefort, J. (2024). *How the energy crisis sped up Europe's green transition*. European Investment Bank. Retrieved December 3, 2024, from https://www.eib.org/en/essays/europe-energy-transition-renewable

Huttunen, S., & Rekola, A. (2021). Reilu siirtymä, ekologinen solidaarisuus ja kestävyysmurroksen mahdollisuus [A just transition, ecological solidarity and the possibility of sustainability transition]. *Alue Ja Ympäristö, 50*(2), 154–164. https://doi.org/10.30663/ay.109042

Kern, K. Grönholm, S., Haupt, W., Hopman, L., Tynkkynen, N., & Kettunen, P. (2021). *Turku is a forerunner in climate mitigation but has catching up to do in climate adaptation*. Research briefings 1–2021. Turku Urban Research Programme Research. Retrieved January 9, 2024, from https://www.turku.fi/sites/default/files/atoms/files/researchbriefings_2021-1.pdf

Martín, C. (2022). Exploring climate change in US housing policy. *Housing Policy Debate, 32*(1), 1–13. https://doi.org/10.1080/10511482.2022.2012030

Martínez-Alier, J., Pascual, U., Vivien, F.-D., & Zaccai, E. (2010). Sustainable de-growth: Mapping the context, criticisms and future prospects of an emergent paradigm. *Ecological Economics, 69*(9), 1741–1747. https://doi.org/10.1016/j.ecolecon.2010.04.017

Martiskainen, M., Schot, J., & Sovacool, B. K. (2021). User innovation, niche construction and regime destabilization in heat pump transitions. *Environmental Innovation and Societal Transitions, 39*, 119–140. https://doi.org/10.1016/j.eist.2021.03.001

Newell, P. (2004). Climate change and development: A tale of two cities. *IDS Bulletin: Climate Change and Development, 35*(3), 120–126. https://doi.org/10.1111/j.1759-5436.2004.tb00145.x

Noordegraaf, M., Douglas, S., Geuijen, K., & Van Der Steen, M. (2019). Weaknesses of wickedness: A critical perspective on wickedness theory. *Policy & Society, 38*(2), 278–297. https://doi.org/10.1080/14494035.2019.1617970

Ohisalo, M. (2018). Koti jokaiselle, pähkinä poliitikoille [A home for everyone, a nut to crack for politicians]. *Politiikka, 60*(4), 331–335.

Riekkinen, V., Saikku, L., Karhinen, S., Aro, R., Helonheimo, T., Peltomaa, J., Pitkänen, K., Lounasheimo, J., Kokkonen, V., & Seppälä, J. (2020). *Kohti hiilineutraalia kuntaa: ilmastoverkoston vaikutus kunnan ilmastotyöhön ja päästöihin [Towards a carbon neutral municipality: The effect of climate network in municipal climate work and emissions]*. Suomen ympäristökeskuksen raportteja 20. SYKE. Retrieved December 12, 2024, from https://helda.helsinki.fi/server/api/core/bitstreams/6c39f87f-fada-4559-ae1b-c60740c4b8a6/content

Scott, I., & Gong, T. (2021). Coordinating government silos: Challenges and opportunities. *Global Public Policy and Governance, 1*(1), 20–38. https://doi.org/10.1007/s43508-021-00004-z

Stagrum, A. E., Andenæs, E., Kvande, T., & Lohne, J. (2020). Climate change adaptation measures for buildings—A scoping review. *Sustainability, 12*(5). https://doi.org/10.3390/su12051721

StatFin (Statistics Finland). (2023). *Total energy consumption decreased by five per cent in 2022*. Energy supply and consumption. Retrieved December 11, 2024, from https://stat.fi/en/publication/cl8lnt36ar51h0duts69hbekz

Stead, D., & de Jong, W. M. (2006). *Practical guidance on institutional arrangements for integrated policy and decision-making*. UN.

Termeer, C. J., Dewulf, A., & Biesbroek, R. (2019). A critical assessment of the wicked problem concept: Relevance and usefulness for policy science and practice. *Policy & Society, 38*(2), 167–179. https://doi.org/10.1080/14494035.2019.1617971

Tosun, J., & Lang, A. (2017). Policy integration: Mapping the different concepts. *Policy Studies, 38*(6), 553–570. https://doi.org/10.1080/01442872.2017.1339239

UNEP (United Nations Environment Programme). (2024). *Why does green economy matter?* Retrieved December 11, 2024, from https://www.unep.org/explore-topics/green-economy/why-does-green-economy-matter

Vierikko, K., Nieminen, H., Salomaa, V., Häkkinen, J., Salminen, J., & Sorvari, J. (2020). *Kiertotalous maankäytön suunnittelussa – Kaavoitus kestävän ja luonnonvaroja säästävän kaupunkiympäristön edistäjänä [Circular economy in land use planning - Zoning as a con-

tributor of sustainable and resourceful urban environment]. Suomen ympäristökeskuksen raportteja 45. SYKE. Retrieved December 18, 2024, from https://helda.helsinki.fi/items/b18dcbcc-2857-4232-b384-b547c6a9f4c6

Wicki, M., & Kaufmann, D. (2022). Accepting and resisting densification: The importance of project-related factors and the contextualizing role of neighborhoods. *Landscape and Urban Planning, 220*, 1–11. https://doi.org/10.1016/j.landurbplan.2021.104350

Open Access This chapter is licensed under the terms of the Creative Commons Attribution 4.0 International License (http://creativecommons.org/licenses/by/4.0/), which permits use, sharing, adaptation, distribution and reproduction in any medium or format, as long as you give appropriate credit to the original author(s) and the source, provide a link to the Creative Commons license and indicate if changes were made.

The images or other third party material in this chapter are included in the chapter's Creative Commons license, unless indicated otherwise in a credit line to the material. If material is not included in the chapter's Creative Commons license and your intended use is not permitted by statutory regulation or exceeds the permitted use, you will need to obtain permission directly from the copyright holder.

Chapter 5
Policy Advice

After being introduced as a concept in Arild Underdal's article *Integrated marine policy: What? Why? How?* (1980), policy integration has gained plenty of attention. Both advocated and questioned, it has become known in a wide range of fields. The preoccupation has extended to and has even overwhelmed areas relevant to our book, such as Finnish climate policy (Kivimaa & Mickwitz, 2009), German climate policy (Beck et al., 2009), the nature of environmental and climate policy integration (Adelle & Russel, 2013), spatial planning (Stead & Meijers, 2009), or housing and wellbeing (McCall et al., 2021). Increasingly, it has been studied in the context of wicked, multidisciplinary problems instead of only environmental ones (Candel & Biesbroek, 2016).

Based on the broad research, it is understandable that there are multiple ways to pursue policy integration, and there are just as many factors challenging its achievement (e.g. Stead & de Jong, 2006). As academics have warned, achieving "full" policy integration should not be counted on to fully solve wicked problems (Candel & Biesbroek, 2016, 225).

One obstacle of policy integration is the incoherence of sectoral policies and outright conflicts between them (Briassoulis, 2004). The issue is to organise multi-level structures so that policy can be achieved through cross-sectoral coordination and cooperation (Behnke & Hegele, 2024). But in a sea of possibilities, there is not one correct solution to policy integration (Stead & Meijers, 2009, 330). This chapter presents some possible ways to advance the integration of climate and housing policies, which were discovered while studying the three Finnish and three German cities. In the form of reflection and questions, we provide policy advice concerning resources, cooperation and policy diffusion, institutional drivers and barriers, topical themes of housing and visioning for the future.

5.1 Ensure Sufficient Financial and Scientific Resources

Sufficient financial resources are often considered a barrier to more sustainable and climate-friendly housing, as ecological housing and construction tend to cost more (e.g. Randolph et al., 2007). This also conflicts with the key challenge and target of housing policy, affordable housing. How can cities reconcile ecologically and socially sustainable housing while also considering emissions and both climate change mitigation and adaptation throughout the apartment's life cycle?

On one hand, money can also be seen as an enabler, pushing developers and markets towards sustainability in the form of different plot competitions or various projects and innovations. On the other hand, many interviewees feel that either rewards or restrictions can encourage developers towards sustainability—and preferably, the choice should be through rewards. It can include taxation and governmental financial support, as seen in how the Finnish government financially supports changing heating systems to more sustainable alternatives. The overall message seems to be that investing now saves money in the long run. Finnish municipal energy companies have proactively taken steps towards more sustainable energy and carbon neutrality (e.g. Turku Energia, 2023). Although it was noted that the negotiations on these measures were not always smooth, many interviewees praised the outcome, showing that initial reluctance can give way to future successes.

The work of civil servants and elected councillors individually and together also impacts the climate and housing sectors. Particularly Finnish interviewees reflected on the role of civil servants and their resourcing. Civil servants should be ensured the sufficient time, money, and staff to do competent and well-founded work.

Since building climate-friendly housing requires more financial resources, the question of whose money is involved and who is spending it arises. Obviously, municipalities are not the only ones producing housing on municipal land, and some interviewees report that municipal housing companies already show broader interest in sustainable construction and housing. Alongside financial drivers, many councillors wish for the city to guide the development and to set certain targets and requirements for the quality and quantity of construction. Norms and policies influence what types of projects are techno-economically executable or reasonable.

In addition to the regulation of construction and housing, municipal governance offers symbolic value: what kind of housing and future we pursue, imagine, and enable. As Antikainen et al. (2020, 14) note, housing policy requires both responsiveness to changing circumstances and long-term planning, as the current issues in housing policy have been present for a long time. These complex—even wicked—problems require consideration of all policy areas connected to housing policy, such as climate or social policy. Municipalities can influence what is built and how; they just have to exercise that power. This also naturally requires local councillors to determine the most sustainable solution from a social, ecological, and holistic perspective, which leads to the question of knowledge. Municipalities can influence sustainable construction and can even create more information on the subject at the same time. In Turku, the municipal housing company TVT executed a project comparing the ecological conditions of concrete and wooden construction (see TVT, 2020). In Kiel, the municipal housing company Kieler Wohnungsgesellschaft (KiWoG) strives for the long-term and sustainable development of its portfolio properties. Additionally, KiWoG focuses on promoting the connection of mobility and housing through the establishment of innovative, integrated, and tenant-friendly mobility concepts (Kieler Wohnungsgesellschaft, 2024).

Even though money emerges as the most important resource, many interviewees also brought up knowledge, which was often described as lacking or uncertain. The amount of information to absorb as a councillor is enormous, and many wonder whether they have all the information on the most sustainable options in the long term or if the "right" calculation methods are even available. As Head (2022, 50–51) points out, evidence-based policymaking has also gained criticism. In the end, knowledge and experts do not solve wicked problems, but the solutions ultimately are under political control. Research data can also be selectively used to promote the personal ideologies of politicians, which is not their intention. Interviewed councillors recognise that data can be used to support their own ideological opinions, e.g. both demolition and refurbishment of older buildings can be justified with science. The question is not only how to extract the right information from the sea of data but also whether all the needed information is there. How can municipalities encourage science, innovation, and experimentation and formulate it in a way that gives answers and support to political action? How can governments attract knowledge and skills to cities and to positions where they will also find their way to decision-makers?

The needs of working life will change with the green/sustainability transition, and they should be met with upgraded skills, training, and education. As a significant step towards more sustainable construction and housing, the circular economy should be strengthened. This could happen through arranging complementary training and education in organisations, making multidisciplinary competence possible, and adapting policy into the changes that circular economy brings to work and competence (Sinervo et al., 2022, 13).

When talking about locally guiding climate-friendly housing and construction, we are challenged with what *climate-friendly* actually means. It should not be reduced to actions that only mitigate climate change, as there is a growing need to account for adaptation. Although predicting future changes is not easy, the studied cities have tried to respond to them. As climate change impacts our physical living environment in the form of floods, heat waves, extreme weather events and other impacts, integrating adaptation into housing policy becomes crucial. Adaptation requires knowledge, support, and education. An example can be found in Denmark, where expert-led workshops and training are being used to support local authorities in their adaptation work (Berninger et al., 2021, 82).

When Finnish municipalities were asked in 2021 about the climate expertise they use, 40% mentioned the expertise of universities, universities of applied sciences, and research institutes (Puurula et al., 2022, 30). Considering the strong emphasis on knowledge-based leadership, the need for knowledge and the challenges in absorbing it, the expertise of universities could be used and shared even more profoundly. As major university cities, Oulu, Turku, and Tampere excel in this respect. Interviewees in Oulu reported on significant cooperation with the university, and in Turku, the city-supported Urban Research Programme successfully creates practical policy advice and observations based on multidisciplinary science (Turku Urban Research Programme, 2024). This type of cooperation with universities can bring informed, city-specific policy advice.

The need for scientific resources is not only related to climate change. As mentioned earlier, wicked problems have been criticised for their "vagueness", which can lead to them being seen as impossible to solve (Noordegraaf et al., 2019). Further research and analysis of wicked problems and their practical solutions could also assist in decision-making on wicked problems (Termeer et al., 2019, 176).

5.2 Advance National and International Policy Diffusion

Neither the German nor the Finnish cities had found a holistic, practical solution to the problem of sustainable housing. With the contextual nature of wicked problems, this makes it impossible to identify a "formula" through which the cities could learn from each other. Nevertheless, sharing successful and challenging experiences between cities and countries has proved to be an important way of promoting sustainable housing.

The interviewees from Turku brought up a field trip to Copenhagen, which had influenced the drafting of the housing policy document at the time. In Germany, some interviewees coincidentally mentioned district heating that had been well implemented in Copenhagen and Denmark in general, and reference was made to facade greening in Barcelona and Rome. The masterplans in Germany were drawn up with the involvement of almost 1000 experts and residents, and the Finnish masterplans are also open to comment by citizens and experts alike. This tells of the payoff of international communication between cities and participative elements.

Finnish municipalities have used cooperation as a practical and prolific form of climate action for some time. In Kuntaliitto's survey, municipalities reported that of all the climate expertise, they rely most (60%) on other municipalities or joint municipal authorities (Puurula et al., 2022, 30), with cooperation estimated as mostly good or very good (67%) (ibid., 20). One formula that has interested many national and international cities is Oulu's success with cycling, as transport has become the main challenge for Finnish municipalities in terms of emissions.

The Finnish HINKU network has successfully spread climate knowledge between municipalities. In their study (Riekkinen et al., 2020, 44), some municipalities had exchanged good practices and experiences outside of the network's formal meetings. Neighbouring municipalities (but also more distant municipalities) that were at the forefront of climate work connected with each other. However, the study found that contact was mainly maintained with the geographically closest municipalities or those that participated in the network. Cooperating with more distant cities, both national and international, outside of the same climate networks could open opportunities. Varying networks, research projects, and environmental reports are useful for exchanging information and functional practices between different sectors, although the comparability of data might prove challenging (Stead & de Jong, 2006, 11).

One characteristic of wicked problems is that they are solved as "one-shot" operations; there is no room for failure because every attempt is significant with possibly heavy consequences. However, the pursuit of a sustainable future is not without its setbacks. While sharing successes and experiences is important, sharing the failed attempts can be equally so. In their article, Heiskanen et al. (2022) discuss a series of events organised in 2018–2019, where pioneers in energy experimentation were given the opportunity to openly share their experiments with failures. In the best-case scenario, this could lead to embracing cultural change and sharing learned information. Events like this bring together actors from different backgrounds, which also enables new networks. Existing climate networks can indeed be used to create an exchange on housing, or a new network could be set up to focus on sustainable housing or the integration of housing and climate policies.

In their report on adaptation, Berninger et al. (2021, 86) call on Finland to bring forward a shared Nordic adaptation policy, which is yet to be created. The similar environmental circumstances and previous, effective cooperation in the Nordic countries may indeed make an ambitious, joint climate policy possible. Although solutions to wicked problems are very contextual as the problems and their solutions are unique, ideas for solutions can be drawn from other cities. It is just as important to adapt the ideas to the specific contexts of cities.

5.3 Explore Institutional Designs Supporting Integration

As is evident from the interviews, some see housing policy as a "patchwork quilt" that could benefit from better communication and a linkage between climate and housing sectors. Institutions have many ways of strengthening the interconnection of housing and climate; one possibility is to "force" the connection by requiring coordinating bodies, cross-cutting committees or establishing a climate commission. Institutional strengthening of the existing climate protection advisory boards in Germany could also be helpful.

Even great policies do not necessarily produce major or long-term benefits due to changing policy objectives or contexts (Head, 2022, 41). Some Finnish councillors expressed concern over the seasonally changing policy and questioned how long-term policies can be made with politicians only having 4 years to make an impact. Although councillors do not wish to bind future generations of decision-makers to long-term policies, it may be somewhat necessary when it comes to climate change. Municipalities do also create long-term plans all the time, for example when constructing new residential areas or schools. Hence, municipalities are capable of other forms of long-term planning. It should be possible to incorporate climate policy into projects since most parties are committed to climate mitigation.

Councillors' knowledge influences the integration of climate policy and housing policy. Sufficient levels of knowledge and expertise can be pursued through training and workshop (Stead & de Jong, 2006, 10). In Turku, the Green interviewees highlighted the rotation principle, which means that representatives can only serve two terms in the same committee position. This allows their knowledge to flow into several positions, which could be a way of facilitating the mutual understanding in integration of sectors. However, it can also be criticised for hindering longer lines in decision-making, as it doesn't allow councillors to build a longer perspective of the issues on their hands.

The nature of wicked problems is that they lack clear, definitive answers, which naturally makes it challenging to solve them. Conklin (2006, 5, referred to in Head, 2022, 56) has argued that rather than finding a final solution, it is important to bring stakeholders together to negotiate towards coherent understanding and possible solutions to the problems.

The active role of Finnish municipalities in pursuing carbon neutrality (Seppälä et al., 2019, 28–29) and the pioneering role of Turku and Tampere in climate work prove that it is possible to be more ambitious in combining housing and climate. However, in the case of the UK, Ross (2010) argues that it is structurally capable of achieving sustainable development, but the lack of a legal basis makes it impossible. Furthermore, sustainability strategies fail to build consensus and integration of conflicting demands. The importance of both international and national regulation becomes apparent. In Finland, the new Construction Act, which will enter into force in 2025, shows potential as it aims to guide construction towards sustainability, digitality, and smoother bureaucratic processes. Internationally, the European Union has a strong influence on sustainable energy practices or circular economy through The European Green Deal. The EU is also currently working on reforming the Construction Products Regulation in a direction that supports the green transition, but the process will take years (European Union, 2023).

5.4 Support Research on the Core Themes of Sustainable Housing

Redensification features strongly in studied housing policy programmes and interviews as a way of making sustainable housing and cities. The climate-friendly effects of redensification are backed by science: they allow the human footprint to be concentrated on nature in the most compact area possible, reducing distances and enabling the most efficient infrastructure possible (Maijala, 2009, referred to in Kerkkänen, 2010, 68). However, the potential negative impacts on climate adaptation, nature and urban aesthetics, or quality of living are just as evident. Kerkkänen (2010, 69) notes that poorly designed, overly intensive redensification can lead to deterioration in the quality and social sustainability of the living environment.

The challenges associated with redensification, such as a concrete-filled urban environment, deteriorating ventilation and the urban heat island effect, must be taken into account at the urban planning and decision-making level. Redensification should be operated so that, for example, fresh air can keep circulating and districts do not lose quality. It should also be accompanied by solutions that promote a pleasant aesthetic urban environment and climate change adaptation, such as greening facades or rooftops. Planning and housing policies benefit from weighing up the multiple aspects of redensification.

Given that all new construction requires large amounts of natural resources and produces emissions, the relationship between new construction and refurbishment should be further observed, and the energy efficiency of old housing should be improved (see Bierwirth, 2021). This links construction to redensification and circular economy. Especially in Finland, sustainable housing is strongly linked to construction materials and techniques, such as wood or ecological concrete. These discussions on new or recycled materials will become even more central to sustainable housing in the future.

As a last resort, climate or ecological compensation can be a way of "maintaining" biodiversity as the damage caused by the construction is compensated by enhancing biodiversity elsewhere. The Finnish Nature Conservation Act includes regulation on voluntary ecological compensation (Finnish Ministry of the Environment, 2024).

5.5 Vision the Future

As Dixon et al. (2018, 779) imply, "a well-crafted and inspiring vision has the capacity to influence the planning of decisions, actions, and behaviours that can inspire change and transform individuals". As interviewees paid little attention to imagining and envisioning the future, it is needed between different sectors and stakeholders. In housing and climate policy, the future is inextricably linked to both sectors. All our policy recommendations so far are also linked to this visioning; *sufficient finances and knowledge* enable the visions and give them scientific base, *policy diffusion and cooperation* give practical inspiration and offer useful practices, and political institutions can choose to allow *long-term planning* or bold, *forward-looking policymaking*. Current issues in *sustainable housing research* are very clearly connected to the future, for example in terms of techniques, materials, and what housing will look like in practice in the future.

Urban planning is an effective way of addressing environmental and social challenges such as climate change or social injustice. Building desirable futures via visions can guide decision-making and planning towards sustainability. However, research has found that cities do not involve sustainability holistically enough in their visions. One way to increase this would be to consider the city's connection with neighbouring areas, creating opportunities for joint and synergistic solutions. In addition, greater public involvement in the visioning process has been identified as useful, and it focuses on an urban-built environment more broadly from a sustainability framework (John et al., 2015).

In their study, Gaffikin and Sterrett (2006) found that visioning offers different possibilities for urban planning, which included imagining the future from a more innovative and inclusive perspective and connecting people to local politics in a diverse way. Visioning allows ordinary citizens to voice their visions beyond the familiar juxtaposition of opposing or approving certain city development. Visioning can also bring different and even marginalised voices to the fore.

In Stockholm, a team of researchers (Bradley et al., 2017) rewrote the City of Stockholm's vision for 2030 from a futurist feminist political ecology perspective. The city officials and citizen groups saw visions as useful in mapping the values on which the visions are built and the kinds of futures pictured. The groups offered suggestions for further development, such as workshops with different participants where the visions created can be contrasted and reflected to further develop the city, or an online tool that offers the opportunity to express visions.

Velicu and Barca (2020) remind us how important it is to reimagine things such socioenvironmental justice or work and its role in a truly sustainable society. This can be applied to housing as well: what will sustainable housing look like in 2060? The reimagination and visions of the future begin with concretism—such as workshops or seminars that can inspire and lead the way.

References

Adelle, C., & Russel, D. (2013). Climate policy integration: A case of déjà vu? *Environmental Policy and Governance, 23*(1), 1–12. https://doi.org/10.1002/eet.1601

Antikainen, J., Pyykkönen, S., Huttunen, J., Soininvaara, I., Laakso, S., & Lönnqvist, H. (2020). *Kaupunkiseutujen ja kuntien asuntopoliittisten ohjelmien arviointi ja kehittäminen* [The evaluation and development of housing policy programmes of city regions and municipalities]. Loppuraportti. MAL-verkosto ja asumisen rahoitus- ja kehittämiskeskus ARA. Retrieved December 12, 2023, from https://mal-verkosto.fi/wp-content/uploads/2020/05/Liite-1.-Kaupunkiseutujen-ja-kuntien-asuntopoliittisten-ohjelmien-arviointi-ja-kehitta%CC%88minen-loppuraportti-MDI-1.pdf

Beck, S. Kuhlicke, S., & Görg, C. (2009). *Climate policy integration, coherence, and governance in Germany. PEER Climate Change Initiative - Project 2: "Climate policy integration, coherence, and governance"*. Retrieved December 12, 2024, from https://www.econstor.eu/bitstream/10419/57858/1/702514535.pdf

Behnke, N., & Hegele, Y. (2024). Achieving cross-sectoral policy integration in multilevel structures—Loosely coupled coordination of "energy transition" in the German "Bundesrat". *The Review of Policy Research, 41*(1), 160–183. https://doi.org/10.1111/ropr.12551

Berninger, K., Tiusanen, M., & Tynkkynen, O. (2021). *Adaptation to climate change in the Baltic Sea and Arctic Regions – Governance and policy tools across countries*. Reports 25. Southwest Finland Centre for Economic Development, Transportation and the Environment. Retrieved March 3, 2024, from https://www.doria.fi/bitstream/handle/10024/181635/Reports%2025%20 2021_.pdf?sequence=1&isAllowed=y

Bierwirth, A. (2021). Wohnraumpolitik versus Umweltpolitik: ein Widerspruch? [Housing policy versus environmental policy: A contradiction?]. In G. Spars (Ed.), *Wohnungsfrage 3.0. Perspektiven auf Gesellschaft und Politik*. W. Kohlhammer GmbH.

References

Bradley, K., Gunnarsson-Östling, U., Schalk, M., & Andreasson, J. (2017). Futurist feminist political ecology – Rewriting Stockholm's Vision 2030. In M. Schalk, T. Kristiansson, & R. Mazé (Eds.), *Feminist futures of spatial practice* (pp. 301–328). Spurbuchverlag.

Briassoulis, H. (2004). *Policy integration for complex policy problems: What, why and how.* Retrieved December 12, 2024, from https://citeseerx.ist.psu.edu/document?repid=rep1&type=pdf&doi=c6094de1b2c3e1988b40f6c8546673a55a925e76

Candel, J. J. L., & Biesbroek, R. (2016). Toward a processual understanding of policy integration. *Policy Sciences, 49*(3), 211–231. https://doi.org/10.1007/s11077-016-9248-y

Conklin, J. (2006). *Dialogue mapping: Building shared understanding of wicked problems.* Wiley.

Dixon, T., Montgomery, J., Horton-Baker, N., & Farrelly, L. (2018). Using urban foresight techniques in city visioning: Lessons from the Reading 2050 vision. *Local Economy, 33*(8), 777–799. https://doi.org/10.1177/0269094218800677

European Union. (2023). *The Commission welcomes provisional agreement on the revised Construction Products Regulation, which strengthens the Single Market and supports the green transition.* Retrieved March 1, 2024, from https://single-market-economy.ec.europa.eu/news/commission-welcomes-provisional-agreement-revised-construction-products-regulation-which-strengthens-2023-12-14_en

Finnish Ministry of the Environment. (2024). *Ecological compensation.* Retrieved March 5, 2024, from https://ym.fi/en/ecological-compensation

Gaffikin, F., & Sterrett, K. (2006). New visions for old cities: The role of visioning in planning. *Planning Theory & Practice, 7*(2), 159–178. https://doi.org/10.1080/14649350600673070

Head, B. W. (2022). *Wicked problems in public policy: Understanding and responding to complex challenges.* https://doi.org/10.1007/978-3-030-94580-0

Heiskanen, E., Happonen, J., Matschoss, K., & Mikkonen, I. (2022). Learning from failures - Encouraging lesson-sharing in the Finnish energy transition. *Energy Research & Social Science, 90*, 102676. https://doi.org/10.1016/j.erss.2022.102676

John, B., Keeler, L. W., Wiek, A., & Lang, D. J. (2015). How much sustainability substance is in urban visions? – An analysis of visioning projects in urban planning. *Cities, 48*, 86–98. https://doi.org/10.1016/j.cities.2015.06.001

Kerkkänen, A. (2010). *Ilmastonmuutoksen hallinnan politiikka - Kansainvälisen ilmastokysymyksen haltuunotto Suomessa [The politics of climate change governance - Reception of the international concern over climate change in Finland].* [Dissertation, University of Tampere]. Acta Electronica Universitatis Tamperensis 995. Tampere: University of Tampere. Retrieved March 7, 2024, from https://trepo.tuni.fi/bitstream/handle/10024/66660/978-951-44-8207-6.pdf?sequence=1&isAllowed=y

Kieler Wohnungsgesellschaft. (2024). *Nachhaltigkeit [Sustainability].* Retrieved March 7, 2024, from https://www.kieler-wohnungsgesellschaft.de/kiwog/nachhaltigkeit/

Kivimaa, P., & Mickwitz, P. (2009). *Making the climate count: Climate policy integration and coherence in Finland.* The Finnish Environment 3 | 2009. Finnish Environment Ministry Research Department. Retrieved December 12, 2024, from https://helda.helsinki.fi/server/api/core/bitstreams/5d0ab573-8613-4253-9dab-6083ec4511b8/content

Maijala, O. (2009). Yhdyskuntarakenteen eheyttäminen ja ekotehokkuus. In R. Sairinen (Ed.), *Yhdyskuntarakenteen eheyttäminen ja elinympäristön laatu* (15–26). Yhdyskuntasuunnittelun tutkimus- ja koulutuskeskuksen julkaisuja B 96.

McCall, V., Hoyle, L., Gunasinghe, S., & O'Connor, S. (2021). A new era of social policy integration? Looking at the case of health, social care and housing. *Journal of Social Policy, 50*(4), 809–827. https://doi.org/10.1017/S0047279420000525

Noordegraaf, M., Douglas, S., Geuijen, K., & Van Der Steen, M. (2019). Weaknesses of wickedness: A critical perspective on wickedness theory. *Policy & Society, 38*(2), 278–297. https://doi.org/10.1080/14494035.2019.1617970

Puurula, J., Hildén, M., Sorvali, J., & Jalonen, P. (2022). *Kuntien ja maakuntien ilmastotyön tilanne 2021 [The situation of municipal and regional climate work in 2021].* Suomen Kuntaliitto.

Randolph, B., Kam, M:, & Graham, P. (2007). *Who can afford sustainable housing?* https://doi.org/10.4324/9781315610757-20

Riekkinen, V., Saikku, L., Karhinen, S., Aro, R., Helonheimo, T., Peltomaa, J., Pitkänen, K., Lounasheimo, J., Kokkonen, V., & Seppälä, J. (2020). *Kohti hiilineutraalia kuntaa: ilmastoverkoston vaikutus kunnan ilmastotyöhön ja päästöihin* [*Towards a carbon neutral municipality: The effect of climate network in municipal climate work and emissions*]. Suomen ympäristökeskuksen raportteja 20. SYKE. Retrieved December 12, 2024, from https://helda.helsinki.fi/server/api/core/bitstreams/6c39f87f-fada-4559-ae1b-c60740c4b8a6/content

Ross, A. (2010). It's time to get serious — Why legislation is needed to make sustainable development a reality in the UK. *Sustainability, 2*(4), 1101–1127. https://doi.org/10.3390/su2041101

Seppälä, J., Saikku, L., Soimakallio, S., Lounasheimo, J., Regina, K., & Ollikainen, M. (2019). *Hiilineutraalius ilmastopolitiikassa – Valtiot, alueet ja kunnat* [*Carbon neutrality in climate policy – States, regions and municipalities*]. Suomen ilmastopaneelin raportti 5a/2019. Retrieved December 8, 2023, from https://ilmastopaneeli.fi/hae-julkaisuja/hiilineutraalius-ilmastopolitiikassa-valtiot-alueet-ja-kunnat/

Sinervo, R., Paajanen, T., Turkki, V., & Herlevi, K. (2022). *10 kiertotalousehdotusta Suomelle* [*10 circular economy proposals to Finland*]. Sitran työpaperi. Retrieved December 8, 2023, from https://media.sitra.fi/app/uploads/2022/06/sitra_10_kiertotalousehdotusta_suomelle.pdf

Stead, D., & de Jong, W. M. (2006). *Practical guidance on institutional arrangements for integrated policy and decision-making.* UN.

Stead, D., & Meijers, E. (2009). Spatial planning and policy integration: Concepts, facilitators and inhibitors. *Planning Theory and Practice, 10*(3), 317–332. https://doi.org/10.1080/14649350903229752

Termeer, C. J., Dewulf, A., & Biesbroek, R. (2019). A critical assessment of the wicked problem concept: Relevance and usefulness for policy science and practice. *Policy & Society, 38*(2), 167–179. https://doi.org/10.1080/14494035.2019.1617971

Turku Energia. (2023). *Turku Energian matka kohti hiilineutraaliutta 2029* [*Turku Energia's journey towards carbon neutrality in 2029*]. Valopilkku. Retrieved December 11, 2024, from https://www.turkuenergia.fi/valopilkku/turku-energian-matka-kohti-hiilineutraaliutta-2029

Turku Urban Research Programme. (2024). *Turku Urban Research Programme*. Retrieved February 12, 2024, from https://www.turku.fi/en/turku-urban-research-programme

TVT. (2020). "Identtiset puu- ja betonikerrostalot vertailussa." ["Comparison of identical wooden and concrete apartment buildings"] *TVT* (website), August 21. Retrieved February 14, 2024, from https://www.tvt.fi/fi/ajankohtaista/arkisto/2020/8/21/identtiset-puu%2D%2Dja-betonikerrostalot-vertailussa/

Underdal, A. (1980). Integrated marine policy: What? Why? How? *Marine Policy, 4*(3), 159–169. https://doi.org/10.1016/0308-597X(80)90051-2

Velicu, I., & Barca, S. (2020). The just transition and its work of inequality. *Sustainability: Science, Practice, & Policy, 16*(1), 263–273. https://doi.org/10.1080/15487733.2020.1814585

References

Open Access This chapter is licensed under the terms of the Creative Commons Attribution 4.0 International License (http://creativecommons.org/licenses/by/4.0/), which permits use, sharing, adaptation, distribution and reproduction in any medium or format, as long as you give appropriate credit to the original author(s) and the source, provide a link to the Creative Commons license and indicate if changes were made.

The images or other third party material in this chapter are included in the chapter's Creative Commons license, unless indicated otherwise in a credit line to the material. If material is not included in the chapter's Creative Commons license and your intended use is not permitted by statutory regulation or exceeds the permitted use, you will need to obtain permission directly from the copyright holder.

Appendix: City Profiles

Turku

Inhabitants (2022)	197,900
Location	Southwest
Water body	Baltic Sea and Aura River
Av. housing rent €/m2 (2012)	11.09
Av. housing rent €/m2 (2022)	14.25
Rent increase	28.5%
Political setup (2023)	National Coalition Party 17, Social Democratic Party 12, The Green League 10, Left Alliance 9, Finns Party 7, Swedish People's Party 3, Centre Party 3, Christian Democrats 1, Other 4

© Åbo Akademis bildbank 2021. Anders Lönnfeldt

Peculiarities

- Higher immigrant population compared to other Finnish cities
- Turku Archipelago and the Baltic Sea create a unique context for the city
- Segregation stands out as a major problem
- New ecological residential areas, Skanssi and Linnanfältti, which strive for more sustainable construction and housing
- A strong student city with two universities
- A mediaeval city whose history must be taken into account when building (archaeological excavations, etc.)
- Geographical challenges, such as muddy ground

Appendix: City Profiles

Situation in housing (main problems)

- Segregation
- Small apartments and a lack of diverse housing
- Taxpayers and students leaving to nearby municipalities in search of more suitable and affordable housing
- Highest relative homelessness rate in the country

Situation in climate (main risks)

- Southwest Finland's climate estimated to become 1.7–5.0 °C warmer in the current century compared to recent decades; the rise depends on (global) emissions[a]
- Risks related to water and water management, such as heavy rainfall and floods (especially seawater flooding)
- Changes in the ecosystem
- Warming temperatures and drought

Policy documents on housing and climate

- *Climate Strategy (2022)*: Climate strategy aims for carbon neutrality by 2029 with different targets. The document presents mitigation action of Turku, which includes a carbon-neutral energy system, sustainable low-carbon transportation, sustainable city structure and construction, climate responsibility in investments and purchases, and strengthening biodiversity. The document also has a section for adaptation and analysis of risks and vulnerability, and a section for the achievability of the climate targets. The strategy was updated in 2022.
- *Housing Strategy (2023)*: Housing strategy aims to create diverse and affordable housing. One main point is dismantling segregation and developing residential areas equally. Other strongly mentioned themes are redensification and constructing near transportation, long-term land policy that maintains growth of the city, and quality of construction and housing. The strategy was updated in 2023.

[a]Ilmasto-opas.fi 2022, accessed on 04.12.2023

Tampere

Inhabitants (2022)	249,060
Location	West
Water body	Lakes and Tammerkoski channel
Av. housing rent €/m2 (2012)	11.73
Av. housing rent €/m2 (2022)	15.19
Rent increase	29.5%
Political setup (2023)	National Coalition Party & Swedish People's Party 17, Social Democratic Party 16, The Green League 11, Finns Party 10, Left Alliance 7, Centre Party 3, Christian Democrats 2, Other 1

© GualdimG, 2014
CC BY-SA 4.0 Deed

Peculiarities

- Tramway and exceptionally good public transport
- Strong growth in recent years, attracting new inhabitants
- Strong student city with the second largest university in Finland
- Ecological residential area Hiedanranta, which aims for more sustainable construction and housing

Situation in housing (main problems)

- Small apartments and a lack of diverse housing
- Strong growth driving up rental costs and challenging housing adequacy, creating a need for new and affordable housing
- Taxpayers fleeing to nearby municipalities for more suitable and affordable housing
- Limited possibilities of redensification
- (Homelessness)

Appendix: City Profiles

Situation in climate (main risks)
- Region of Tampere estimates that average annual temperatures will rise by 4 °C[a]
- Increase in rainfall, which can lead to floods
- Increased heat, heatwaves, and drought
- Mild winters contribute to icy conditions and lead to freezing–melting cycles
- Changes in ecosystems related to endangered or protected species (such as Siberian flying squirrel)

Main policy documents on housing and climate
- *Climate Strategy (2022)*: Climate strategy is divided into five sectors that all present goals, measurements, and ways to achieve climate-neutrality by 2030. Sectors are (0) Coordination of climate work (intersects with all the sectors), (1) Sustainable city development, (2) Sustainable transportation system, (3) Sustainable construction, (4) Sustainable energy, (5) Sustainable consuming, and (6) Sustainable city nature. This 2022 update of the document includes measures of climate adaptation.
- *Housing Strategy (2022)*: Housing strategy is divided into nine objectives, which together create a diverse, affordable, high-quality, and sustainable housing policy. Shortened objectives are (1) Enough housing to maintain growth, (2) Diverse housing, (3) Socially sustainable residential areas, (4) Affordable housing, (5) Quality of housing, (6) Housing answering to special needs, (7) Climate policy and biodiversity in housing and land policy, (8) Long-term and responsible land management, and (9) Housing contributes to economic policy.

[a]Hiilineutraali Pirkanmaa, accessed on 04.12.2023

Oulu

Inhabitants (2022)	211,848
Location	Northwest
Water body	Bothnian Bay and river Oulujoki
Av. housing rent €/m2 (2012)	10.51
Av. housing rent €/m2 (2022)	13.17
Rent increase	+25.3%
Political setup (2023)	National Coalition Party 18, Centre Party 13, Finns Party 9, Left Alliance 9, The Green League 8, Social Democratic Party 8, Christian Democrats 1, Other 1

© Gálaniitoluodda, 2020
CC0 1.0

Peculiarities

- Less densely populated than Turku and Tampere
- Rental costs are quite low
- "The cycling capital of Finland"
- A student city
- Ecological and innovative residential areas Hiukkavaara and Hartaanselkä, which aim for more sustainable construction and housing
- Municipality mergers in 2013, when the larger municipality Oulu and four other municipalities merged into "New Oulu"
- Geographical challenges, such as colder temperature

Appendix: City Profiles

Situation in housing (main problems)

- Small apartments and a lack of diverse housing
- Withering city centre
- Amount of accessible and communal housing when the population is ageing

Situation in climate (main problems)

- Increase in annual rainfall (and snowfall occurring as rainfall), which affects the risk of flooding
- Increase in heat and drought
- Mild winters contributing to icy conditions, freezing–melting cycles and darkness, which are health risks
- Effects on agriculture and forestry

Main policy documents on housing and climate

- *Climate Strategy (2019)*: Climate strategy is divided into four different sectors that aim towards carbon neutrality by 2035. All sectors include different goals, action, and measurements, which are used to follow the progression of the climate/environment strategy. The sectors are (1) Sustainable growth (including city structure), (2) Resource-wise action and energy, (3) Nature, and (4) Environment/climate responsibility.
- *Housing and Land Use Strategies (2017 & 2022)*: Housing strategies focus on affordable housing, housing supply to be in line with demand, enough different types of housing (rental, ownership), housing for special groups, redensification, diverse housing and avoiding segregation, and tackling homelessness.

Kiel

Inhabitants (2022)	247,700
Location within the country	North
River/Coast	Coast
Av. housing rent €/m2 (2012)	6.48
Av. housing rent €/m2 (2022)	9.64
Rent increase	+48.8%
Political setup (2023)	Green Party 14, Christian Democrats 11, Social Democrats 11, SSW (Danish Minority) 4, The Left/The Party 3, AfD 3, Independent 3

© Marvin Radke
CC BY-SA 4.0 Deed

Peculiarities

- State capital of Schleswig-Holstein
- Large immigration (especially from students → by 2025: growth of 10,000 inhabitants)
- By 2050, population expected to increase up to 280,000 → "a growing city"
- Coastline creates a unique context for the city
- Port city described as a bridge to Scandinavia and the Baltic States
- Kiel's port functions as a destination for cruise ships, ferry lines, and cargo ships

Appendix: City Profiles

Situation in housing (main problems)

- Lack of (affordable) housing (rent costs are very high; not enough buildings)
- Need for 9000 apartments by 2030.
- Two large corporations (Vonovia, LEG) controlling the housing market
- New (municipal) housing company with limited responsibilities for manoeuvre on infrastructure, the condition, and the rent costs
- Limited expansion possibilities due to its location
- Many old/listed buildings
- Prices, condition, and size of apartments are a major problem because they are usually comparatively large, but only a few people live in them
- Requirements for listed buildings make refurbishment only possible to a limited extent and have a negative impact on prices

Situation in climate (main problems)

- Temperature increases compared to the beginning of the twentieth century already detected today but are low at 0.4 °C compared to 1.2 degrees in Southern Germany
- Annual mean temperature in Schleswig-Holstein expected to increase by between 2 and 4 degrees by 2100
- Extreme dryness and drought: drought-resistant plants and trees planted in Kiel, and slow runoff systems promoted
- Heavy rain risk maps developed because of heavy rainfall events in the past

Main policy documents on housing and climate

- *Climate Masterplan (2017)*: Climate masterplan presents a target by 2050: Reduce greenhouse gas emissions by at least 95% by 2050 compared to 1990 levels, and halve final energy consumption by 2050 compared to 1990 levels.
- *Housing Concept (2020)*: Housing concept includes sustainable housing construction, active land policy, redensification, and potential in existing buildings.

Mainz

Inhabitants (2022)	220,550
Location within the country	West
River/Coast	River
Av. housing rent €/m2 (2012)	8.80
Av. housing rent €/m2 (2022)	12.34
Rent increase	+40.2%
Political setup (2023)	Christian Democrats 14, Social Democrats 12, Green Party 19, Free Democrats 4, The Left 4, AfD 3, Ecological Democrats 2, Free Voters 1, The Party 1

©ekeidar
CC BY-SA 3.0 Deed

Appendix: City Profiles

Peculiarities
- State capital of Rhineland-Palatinate
- Forms a "cross-state double centre" with a common city boundary with Wiesbaden
- Old town with half-timbered houses and mediaeval marketplaces
- Attractive place to work, as many companies like BioNTech are based there
- Student City: University of Mainz is one of the largest German universities
- Known as one of the "growing cities" in Germany
- Location on the Rhine and in the Rhine-Main metropolitan area makes it attractive for tourists
- BioNTech's economic success helping to resolve debt and is known worldwide
- Access to the most important waterways in Germany
- Container port of considerable size that, as a connecting point between inland shipping, rail and road transport, offers ideal conditions for the international transport of goods
- Climate Protection Advisory Council

Situation in housing (main problems)
- Rapidly rising rents in the last 10 years due to the increased population; on the ranking list of German cities with the most expensive rents
- Housing control centre
- Many old/listed buildings
- Shortage of living space and affordable housing
- Faces increasing gentrification
- A lot of unused industrial space that could be used for housing

Situation in climate (main problems)
- An expected significant increase in summer days, hot days and nights by 2060.
- Extreme weather events with heavy rainfalls and floods more probable in the future
- The river carries little water, and this poses a danger to wildlife

Main policy documents on housing and climate
- *Climate Plan (2021)*: Climate plan includes insulation and energy-efficient refurbishment of almost all buildings; efficient heating with solar and environmental heat; comprehensive funding and advisory programmes (refurbishment, energy efficiency, energy generation).
- *Climate Masterplan (2017)*: Climate masterplan has a target to reduce greenhouse gas emissions by at least 95% by 2050 compared to 1990, while at the same time reducing final energy consumption by 50%.
- *Housing Concept (2019)*: Housing concept refers to climate-friendly new construction and conversion of apartments, designing energy-efficient refurbishment in a socially acceptable way, with 5500 new flats by 2025 (more publicly subsidised housing climate-friendly).

Wiesbaden

Inhabitants (2022)	280,000
Location within the country	West
River/Coast	River
Av. housing rent €/m2 (2012)	8.44
Av. housing rent €/m2 (2022)	10.81
Rent increase	+28.1%
Political setup (2023)	Christian Democrats 19, Green 17, Social Democrats 17, Free Democrats 8, The Left 5, AfD 5, Volt 3, Free Voters/Pro Auto 3, Citizens' List 3, Independent 1

© Martin Kraft
CC BY-SA 3.0 Deed

Peculiarities

- State Capital of Hesse
- Second largest city in Hesse after Frankfurt
- A popular place to live → One of the most expensive cities in Germany regarding terms of rents and real estate prices
- Forms a "cross-state double centre" with a common city boundary with Mainz
- The most important military base of the American Forces in Europe
- Historical city with a large proportion of old buildings
- Geological feature: outcrop of thermal and mineral water that emerges from great depths in several places
- High groundwater levels are also expected in the city centre, which has made construction difficult
- Moderate population growth

Appendix: City Profiles

Situation in housing (main problems)

- Lack of affordable housing is a major problem
- The contrast between people with high and low incomes more pronounced due to the city's image as a city of civil servants and spa resorts
- Listed buildings cause problems concerning refurbishment and modernisation measures
- Hilly geographic aspect of Wiesbaden leads to special problems when it comes to construction, such as the fresh-air corridors or heavy rainfall events

Situation in climate (main problems)

- Long dry heat waves
- Damage to road surfaces by the so-called blow-ups
- Agricultural sector: crop failures due to drought
- Bare areas in the urban forest due to the bark beetle in spruce stands becoming increasingly larger
- Forest and field fires due to drought
- The river carries little water, and this poses a danger to wildlife

Main policy documents on housing and climate

- *Integrated Climate Protection Concept (2015)*: Climate protection concept aims to reduce total energy consumption by 20% by 2020 compared to 1990 and the share of renewable energies to be increased to 20%. Reduction potentials in urban development (including new development areas, conversion areas, redensification, urban development and energy-efficient neighbourhood refurbishment) → new construction areas with optimal energy standards and supply; conversion areas with guidelines for new construction apply if new construction can be realised on the conversion areas; refurbish existing buildings in an energy-efficient manner; Neighbourhood-oriented approaches that establish links to the policy field of transport and consumption as well as to climate adaptation and open space quality are important strategic approaches, especially in existing areas.

The manufacturer's authorised representative in the EU is Springer Nature Customer Service Centre GmbH, Europaplatz 3, 69115 Heidelberg, Germany. If you have any concerns regarding our products, please contact ProductSafety@springernature.com

Printed and bound by CPI Group (UK) Ltd, Croydon, CR0 4YY

23/03/2026

02076360-0005